Creative WALL DECORATING

Cover pictures: (l) Elizabeth Whiting &
Associates/Brian Harrison; (tr) Homes &
Gardens/Robert Harding Syndication; (br)
Eaglemoss/Steve Tanner.

Page 1: Abode UK; Page 3: Country Homes &
Interiors/Robert Harding Syndication; Page 4:
Eaglemoss Publications/Steve Tanner; Page 5: Woman
& Home/PWA International.

Based on *Creating Your Home*, published in the UK
© Eaglemoss Publications Ltd 1996
All rights reserved

First published in the USA in 1996
by Betterway Books,
an imprint of F&W Publications Inc.,
1507 Dana Avenue,
Cincinnati, Ohio 45207.

ISBN 1-55870-415-9

Manufactured in Hong Kong

10 9 8 7 6 5 4 3 2 1

Creative
WALL
DECORATING

BETTERWAY BOOKS

Contents

UNIQUE WALLCOVERING TREATMENTS

HANG IT UP

DECORATE WITH TILES

INDEX

SPONGE PAINTING

The soft, mottled pattern produced by sponging a second layer of paint over a base coat adds a stylish broken colour effect to the walls of a room and decorative interest to accessories.

S ponging is an easy, instant paint effect that gives a pleasing, mottled appearance to a surface. As the name implies, the technique involves using a sponge to apply one or more colours to a solid base colour. The final look will depend on the number of coats of paint sponged on – the more there are, the denser the effect – and, most importantly, the colours used. With two close shades of the one colour, the effect is very subtle – from a distance the colours will merge yet not look as flat as an area painted in one colour. If two, or even three, quite different colours are layered the effect is more dramatic.

Because it is such a simple, quick technique, sponging is ideal for covering large expanses of wall, but it also works well on smaller surfaces such as a blanket box, a wall panel or a cupboard door. A more practical advantage of the technique is that it helps disguise obtrusive pipes and radiators. Experiment with different sponge effects on scrap paper before you start work – the following pages show you the basic techniques and there are suggestions for small creative projects.

As well as adding overall interest to a plain expanse of wall, sponging can be used for dramatic creative effects. This bold scheme is made even richer with panels of gold sponged over the red base coat.

SPONGING TECHNIQUE

Emulsion (latex) is the best choice for sponging walls – it is low odour, fairly inexpensive and easy to use, and the base coat can be applied with a roller. In general, two or more sponged colours give a more pleasing effect than one – using just one colour can sometimes look spotty unless the sponged colour is closely related to the base coat. Always try out various colourways on paper before starting work on a project – hold the paper samples up to the wall to test the result.

The sponge you use also affects the final look. Natural sea sponges are best; they are expensive but they produce a wonderfully varied pattern which isn't possible to imitate using a synthetic sponge. However, synthetic sponges are cheaper and more readily available. If you use a synthetic sponge, tear it into an irregular shape and apply the paint with the inner surface.

For a particularly subtle effect, you can dilute the sponging paint with water – test this out on your sample. And if you apply too much paint, remedy the effect by lifting off some of the excess with a dry sponge.

SPONGING ON WALLS

YOU WILL NEED
- ❖ EMULSION (LATEX) PAINTS
- ❖ ROLLER
- ❖ ROLLER TRAY
- ❖ RUBBER GLOVES
- ❖ SPONGE
- ❖ LINING or SCRAP PAPER

1 Testing the result To make sure that the colours you have chosen work well together, first test the effect on a piece of scrap paper or wallpaper lining paper.

2 Painting the base coat Check that the walls are sound and well prepared. Apply one coat of paint with a roller and allow to dry. If the colour underneath was dark, you may need to paint on another base coat and allow to dry. Clean the roller tray thoroughly.

3 Loading the sponge Condition a new sponge by soaking it in water, then wringing it out. Pour some of the second colour into the tray and dip the sponge lightly into it. To achieve the right soft speckled mark, and avoid paint runs, don't allow the sponge to soak up too much paint – it should be almost dry. Blot off any excess on scrap paper or the ridged surface of the tray.

4 Sponging on colour Working from the top of the wall, dab the sponge lightly over the surface. Turn the sponge as you work to vary the pattern. If you are sponging with just one colour, keep the marks as close together as possible for an overall, even effect. If you are using two or more colours you can space them out a little more. Avoid overlaps, especially at corners and beside doors or windows where paint can build up.

5 Adding another colour (optional) Rinse out the sponge thoroughly. Wait for the paint to dry, then apply the second sponged coat over the first, filling in any gaps between the first colour yet still allowing some of the base colour to show through.

◀ *Three different shades of soft deep yellow, shown below, were used for the broken paint effect on this stylish wall. For an extra impression of depth, two colours were sponged over the base coat – if you don't want a build-up of colour, one colour sponged over the base coat may be enough.*

T I P
SPONGING AWKWARD AREAS

When sponging narrow areas such as door or window frames, avoid getting paint on the surrounding area by using a sponging off technique. Use a brush, not a sponge, to apply the second colour over the base coat. Then dab a clean sponge over the wet paint to remove some of the colour.

9

SPONGING TILES

Sponging ceramic tiles is a simple way to give a fresh look to a bathroom or kitchen wall, or to disguise unattractive tiling. The finish described below is hardwearing enough for most bathroom or kitchen tiles, but is not suitable for the tiling around a shower or any other area that will be constantly damp. In this bathroom one colour was sponged over plain white tiles, and a second was sponged on top in a diagonal pattern using a square cut out of card as a template.

It is important to clean the tiles and the grouting thoroughly and leave them to dry out before you apply the paint. Use a solvent/oil-based eggshell paint for sponging over tiles – it has good covering power, and does not need an undercoat. If you are sponging over patterned tiles, or you want a base colour that's different from the original colour of the tiles, prepare the surface as described below then cover the tiles with a base coat of solvent/oil-based gloss or eggshell. Work in a ventilated room when applying solvent-based paints; clean all equipment with white (mineral) spirit.

YOU WILL NEED

- ❖ METHYLATED SPIRIT/ DENATURED ALCOHOL
- ❖ SOFT CLOTHS
- ❖ SOLVENT/OIL-BASED EGGSHELL PAINT
- ❖ ROLLER TRAY
- ❖ SPONGE
- ❖ SCRAP PAPER
- ❖ WHITE (MINERAL) SPIRIT
- ❖ CARDBOARD
- ❖ RULER AND PENCIL
- ❖ CRAFT KNIFE

These bathroom tiles have a new look with a stylish diamond pattern.

1 **Cleaning the surface** Wash the tiles down thoroughly with soap and water and leave for at least 24 hours to dry.

2 **Preparing for painting** To remove any residue of grease and evaporate all remaining moisture off the surface, wipe over the tiles carefully with a little methylated spirit (denatured alcohol) applied to a soft cloth, paying particular attention to the grouting.

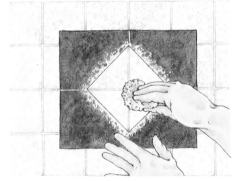

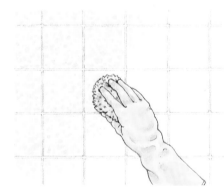

3 **Sponging** Pour a little paint into the tray, and spread out to a thin layer. Dab the sponge into the paint; remove any excess and test the effect on scrap paper. Carefully dab on over the tiles. Leave the paint to dry but clean out tray and sponge at once.

ＴＩＰ

SPONGED BORDER

As a small first-time sponging project, experiment with a sponged border to add interest to plain tiles. Using the same sponge technique as above, cut out a shape from card, and sponge directly through it on to the tiles.

4 **Sponging diagonals** Using a craft knife, cut out a square from the card, with the sides equal to the tile diagonal – the square will provide a template for the sponged diamond shapes. For accurate positioning, mark the continuation of the grout lines on the card. Sponge colour through the square template – if necessary, avoid smudging by sponging alternate diamonds .

COLOURWASHING

The subtle blending of translucent washes of colour gives walls an appealingly soft and weathered character which is traditionally associated with a natural country style.

Created by quickly applying one or two thin washes of colour over a base coat, colourwashing is suitable for rooms of all shapes and sizes. A rich depth can be achieved with deep colours, while soft colourwashing provides an ideal background for wallpaper borders and other decorating techniques such as stencilling and block printing.

One of the main advantages of colourwashing is that it's really easy to get a pleasing result. All you need is emulsion (latex) paint, brushes and water. The technique is ideal for walls that are uneven or in poor condition, as any imperfections merge in to become part of the finish. And if you are dissatisfied with the colour of a newly painted wall, a colourwash technique is quicker and uses less paint than painting the wall again in the ordinary way. All that you need do is cover the painted wall with a thinned wash of a coordinating or contrasting colour.

A wash of yellow over a white base coat brings a hint of sunshine into a room.

COLOURWASHING A WALL

To colourwash walls, a thin wash of diluted paint, normally emulsion (latex), is brushed in all directions over a base coat of dried paint.

For the wash you can use a colour that tones or contrasts with the base coat, depending on the effect you want to achieve. Generally, colourwashing works best where the wash is a slightly darker shade than the base coat.

The colourwashing technique is very simple. When brushing on the colourwash, you need to apply enough pressure to leave brush marks that show up clearly. A dry brush is then lightly stroked over the wet paint to soften and blur the original brush marks and reveal the background colour. The more you brush out the wet paint, the more subtle the colourwash will be.

One wash of colour over the base coat is usually enough to achieve the right effect, but for greater depth you can build up the colour by using two different coloured washes. To do this, brush out and soften the first wash while it's still wet, then allow it to dry completely before applying the next. Don't attempt to use more than two colourwashes over the base coat, or you're likely to lose the lovely translucence of the wash.

Before you start painting a wall, it's a good idea to buy some tester pots of paint and experiment with different colour mixes on a large sheet of lining paper. Stick the paper on the wall with masking tape to check the result in both day and artificial light.

It's also sensible to wear old clothes when you're colourwashing – it can be a messy business.

CHOOSING COLOURS

Soft pale colours have a carefree, country cottage feel and usually look best applied over a white background. In a cool sunless room, create a sun-dappled effect by using bright yellow, coral or pink. Try cool tones of aqua, moss green or hydrangea blue in a warm sunny room.

Dark colours produce strong, sophisticated effects, but as the paint is applied thinly the colour is unlikely to be overpowering. Try a pastel base with two rich colours over it. Be bold with your choice of colours – paint a pale pink wall with magenta, for example, and add a scarlet wash, or experiment with emerald green over turquoise.

1 Applying the base colour Protect the floor and nearby furniture with plastic sheets or newspaper, then use a roller or paint brush to paint the walls with a matt emulsion base coat. Allow to dry and add a second coat of the same colour. Leave to dry overnight.

2 Mixing the wash To thin the colourwash emulsion so that the colour beneath shows through, dilute one part paint to four parts water in the paint kettle.

3 Applying the wash Dip the brush into the wash and remove excess with a rag. Working quickly on a 1.2m (4ft) square of wall, brush on the diluted paint from every direction in large sweeping movements.

4 Softening the brush strokes Using a dry brush, work over the wet section of wall to blur or remove any hard and obvious brush marks. Dry the brush regularly by wiping it on a rag.

THE PROFESSIONAL FINISH

For a more translucent, tougher **finish** than emulsion (latex), try colourwashing with a special solvent/oil-based scumble glaze which is available from art supply shops. You can use the glaze on all interior walls and woodwork, but as it's more expensive than emulsion and is very durable, it's particularly suitable for colourwashing a small area that comes in for heavy wear, such as a door. Because of its base, a scumble glaze would also suit a condensation-prone zone such as a bathroom or kitchen. To use the glaze, dilute with white (mineral) spirit and colour it by adding solvent/oil-based eggshell. For a base coat use solvent/oil-based eggshell, or vinyl silk emulsion (satin latex) for areas of less heavy wear.

A pale wash of cool sea-blue over white gives translucent depth to this wall. All you need for this sort of colourwashing is emulsion (latex) paint and water, and the technique couldn't be simpler. The wash is vigorously swept over the surface and then brushed out to reveal some of the base colour.

5 Checking the effect When you have completed a section, stand back and make sure that the paint is evenly dispersed. If you want to reveal more base colour, go over the wet paint again, using firm strokes with the dry brush to remove more paint. Continue across the wall, applying the wash and softening the brush strokes as you work, and making sure that you soften and blend in adjoining sections. Finish by brushing out excess paint at the edges of the wall, in corners or around doors and windows.

6 Adding more colour (optional) To add more depth and shade to the wall, wait until the first wash has dried then apply a second wash in a different colour. Simply repeat steps 2, 3, 4 and 5.

TIP

SOFTENING THE EFFECT
For a softer overall effect, use a dry piece of cotton rag to wipe away the colourwash and blur the brush strokes. Follow steps 1-3, then fold a clean rag into a loose pad to wipe the wet wall, using a mixture of dabbing and light rubbing movements. Because the amount of base coat revealed can be more carefully controlled than with a brush, the rag method is especially useful for a small area such as a door.

PAINTING A BLANKET BOX

If you want to experiment with colourwashing but would rather begin with a small project, try your hand at painting a piece of wooden furniture like a blanket box or small cupboard.

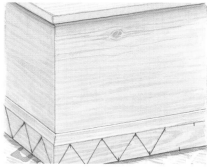

A wash of soft green emulsion over a base coat of pale blue, combined with a cheerful zigzag border, gives a new lease of life to a blanket box. A name picked out in border colours on the lid is a nice personal touch.

1 Preparing the box Protect the working area with plenty of plastic sheets or newspaper, then sand smooth any painted or varnished surfaces on the box and fill any cracks with wood filler. Sand smooth again and wipe off dust with a cloth. If necessary, apply white wood primer to seal any bare wood.

2 Marking off the border Measure and mark a pencil line all round the box about 10cm (4in) from the base. Mark alternate equal distances along the line and the base of the box and join up the points in a zigzag pattern. Cover the top of the border with masking tape.

3 Applying the paint Brush a base coat of pale blue over the whole box, stopping at the masking tape. Leave to dry. Dilute one part green paint with four parts water and brush the wash quickly all over the base coat down to the masking tape.

4 Softening the lines Using a dry brush or cotton rag, work over the painted surfaces to soften the brush strokes and reveal some of the base coat.

5 Wiping the edges Wrap a clean cloth tightly around your forefinger then, using your nail to create a sharp edge, wipe the wash off the edge of the lid and the strip above the border. Wipe smoothly and cleanly, trying not to smudge the colourwash, then leave to dry.

6 Painting in the pattern Remove the masking tape from the base and use the smaller brush to paint in the triangles with different coloured paint. Don't worry if the lines between the colours are not completely straight and crisp – soft lines only add to the charm.

BLOCK PRINTING

*The simplest of printing methods, block printing
makes ingenious use of everyday materials to add pattern and colour
to walls and accessories around your home.*

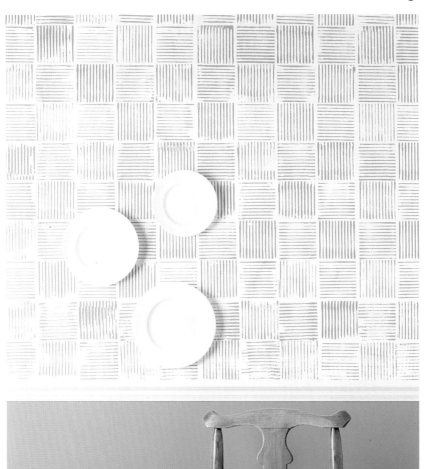

W ith its pleasant, handcrafted look, block printing is a fun way of creating patterns or adding a texture to items around your home. The block simply describes the item that you print with – traditionally it would have been a motif carved out of a wooden block, but it is possible to improvise. A shape can be carved out of the surface of soft materials such as sponge or potatoes, or a textured material mounted on to a wooden block. Then you simply apply paint to the block and stamp your design directly on to the surface to be decorated.

Part of the fun of block printing lies in experimenting with different materials. Many objects commonly found around the house can be used – try the end of a cork from a bottle, a sponge, an offcut of carpet, old table mat, corrugated cardboard or even scraps of textured wallpaper. Some materials, such as wallpaper, need to be mounted on to a small block of wood or sanding block so that they are easy to hold while printing; others, like a sponge, work well without a block.

Pleasing and dramatic effects can be created by using just one colour. And, as handprinting is always irregular, don't worry if each print is slightly different, as any variations will add to the final effect. Walls, furniture, accessories or fabric can be decorated this way, whether you print the entire item with repeated motifs, print just one motif or create a border. Before you start, experiment first on scrap paper.

*You can achieve a stylish result at little
cost and with the simplest of materials
– here, prints from corrugated
cardboard taped to a wooden
block create a pleasing
chequerboard effect.*

PRINTING TECHNIQUES

The basic techniques of block printing are the same whatever you choose to print and use as a block. The steps below show printing with a sponge – if you use a material that needs to be mounted on a block, prepare the block first then proceed with the steps. Always mark out and prepare the area to be painted with care, and make a few practice prints on scrap paper. Protect your finished design with a coat of varnish.

SUITABLE PAINTS

Many paints can be used for block printing – but for the best results the paint should be the consistency of thick cream. Special block printing paints are available from artists' supply shops. These have the right creamy consistency and do not dry too quickly on the block, so they give a well defined print. Artist's acrylics and children's PVA paints are suitable and it is also possible to use water-based household paints such as matt emulsion (flat latex). Tester pots of emulsion are an ideal size for first time or small scale projects.

MAKING A BLOCK

Blocks can be made by carving into the surface of wood, lino or materials such as sponge or potato. Alternatively, mount soft items such as string or carpet, or those which cannot be easily held, on to a separate piece of wood using a waterproof glue. Pliable materials, such as textured wallpaper or card, can be wrapped around a block and taped in place.

APPLYING THE PAINT

One of the best ways of applying the paint to the block is with a small roller, from an art shop, which coats the paint evenly over the surface. A brush can be used, but not as effectively. Or you can dip the block into a dish of paint – this is the easiest way to coat soft surfaces such as sponge, but dab off excess paint on scrap paper before printing.

▶ *A simple chequerboard sponge print sealed with several coats of varnish makes a handsome splashback to this sink – follow the steps below to experiment with the technique.*

PREPARING THE SURFACE

The surface must be sound, clean and free of grease. Wash down walls or furniture with a mild solution of (sugar) soap or detergent, and allow them to dry thoroughly before printing. If the paint is flaking or peeling it should be removed and the surface repainted.

SPONGE PRINTING

A household synthetic sponge can be used as a square as shown here, or carved into shapes with a craft knife. The steps show a chequerboard effect being practised on a sheet of card.

> **YOU WILL NEED**
>
> ❖ RULE, PENCIL
> ❖ MASKING TAPE
> ❖ SYNTHETIC SPONGE cut into a 15cm (6in) square
> ❖ EMULSION (LATEX) PAINT, in blue or colour of your choice
> ❖ OLD PLATE large enough to take the sponge
> ❖ SCRAP PAPER
> ❖ CLEAR, water-based VARNISH and BRUSH

1 Positioning the design Use a rule and pencil to work out where you want the first row of squares to start. Mark this position with masking tape.

2 Positioning the motifs Using the sponge as a template, mark off the position of the chequer pattern along the edge of the masking tape.

3 Applying the paint Pour a small amount of paint on to the plate. Lightly press the sponge into the paint and dab off any excess on to scrap paper.

4 Making prints Working from just above the tape upwards, press the sponge on the card, matching the corners to the guide marks. Re-apply the paint if necessary, then print again, a blank square away from the first one. Print the first row then continue the chequer pattern by alternating the order of printed squares in each row.

5 Finishing When the design has dried, apply two or three coats of clear, water-based varnish, allowing it to dry completely between coats.

PRINT EFFECTS

As a first time project, try your hand on something small such as a tray, blanket box, border or frieze. Simple geometric patterns often work best – as your skills develop you may want to progress to a more complex, freer style of design.

▶ *Dramatic in its simplicity, this handpainted yellow border has been sponge printed with rectangles in a contrasting colour.*

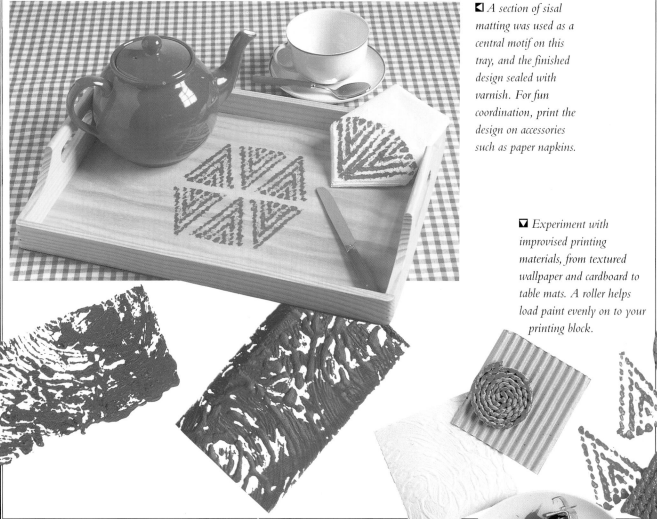

◀ *A section of sisal matting was used as a central motif on this tray, and the finished design sealed with varnish. For fun coordination, print the design on accessories such as paper napkins.*

▶ *Experiment with improvised printing materials, from textured wallpaper and cardboard to table mats. A roller helps load paint evenly on to your printing block.*

PAINTING STRIPES

Painted stripes add impact to walls and make a lively change from plain backgrounds. They're easy to paint if you use masking tape to guide you along the edges.

Depending on the colours, proportions and paint finish, painted stripes on walls can give a number of different effects – from subtle, classic and elegant to bold, jazzy and modern. You can use bright, clashing colours or mellow, toning combinations, either applied as flat colour or with a paint effect, such as sponging, dragging or stippling, for a softer finish.

Really dramatic striped effects are best reserved for less frequently used rooms, such as dining rooms, where you can enjoy them without having to live with them all day, or for children's rooms where they'll create a fun, stimulating

backdrop. Subtler looks, such as honey beige stripes over a cream base, fit in anywhere.

For the look to succeed, the stripes need to be absolutely vertical or horizontal, and perfectly parallel. You can achieve this with careful measuring and marking up, using a plumb line for vertical stripes and a level for horizontal ones. For the neatest outline, use masking tape to define the edges of the stripes. If you live in an old house, take a good look at the walls before you begin – if they're very irregular and slope at the corners, you might need to reconsider using stripes as they emphasize any imperfections.

If you find all-over striped walls a trifle overpowering, opt for a stripy dado instead. In this sunny bedroom, wide lilac stripes painted over a green-grey base coat and topped with a horizontal band of peach give the dado the feeling of a balustrade.

Painting Stripes on to a Wall

You Will Need

- ❖ Filler
- ❖ Emulsion (Latex) Paint – one colour for the base coat and one or two other shade(s) for the stripes
- ❖ Roller to apply base coat
- ❖ Plumb Line
- ❖ Measuring Tape
- ❖ Chalk
- ❖ Masking Tape
- ❖ Sponge
- ❖ Small Paint Brush
- ❖ Craft Knife

When measuring and marking up the stripes, try to arrange them symmetrically around features such as fireplaces and windows to achieve a balanced effect. The easiest way to do this is to centre the first stripe then work out from it.

These steps are for vertical stripes sponged in two colours over the base coat, but are easily adapted for horizontal stripes. To mark up horizontal stripes, measure and mark down from the ceiling at several points to the height of the first key stripe. Join the marks using a level and straightedge. Measure up and down from this line for the other stripes.

▶ For details on sponging, see pages 7-10.

Planning a Design

It's a good idea to plan your striped design before you begin. To make masking off easier, make the base colour stripes the same width as your masking tape – usually 2.5cm (1in), though you can buy wider widths. Also, if you leave a space between every painted stripe, as shown here, you only need to mask off the spaces – not the stripes themselves.

Draw a section of the design to scale on a large piece of paper and colour it in. Hold it up to the wall to check the effect. If it's a bold design, leave it there for a few days to make sure you don't tire of it.

1 Applying the base coat Prepare the walls, filling any cracks and holes. Use the roller to apply the base coat, then leave it to dry thoroughly.

2 Marking up the stripes Measure the width of the wall (or of the feature on which you want to centre the stripes) and mark the mid-point. Hang a plumb line from the ceiling at this point. Use the chalk to mark small dots on to the wall at intervals down the plumb line. This line indicates the *centre* of your first stripe. Following your design, measure and mark out from the dots on each side to mark up the stripe widths across the wall, using a plumb line at intervals to check the stripes are vertical.

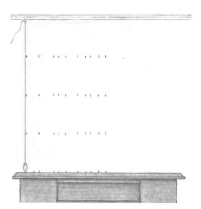

3 Dealing with corners As you work towards the corners, plan ahead to make sure you have a full stripe on each side; this often involves making slight adjustments to the width of the stripes running up to the corner, but this won't be noticeable in the end result.

4 Masking off Use masking tape to mask off the stripes you want to remain the base colour, lining up the tape edges with the chalk dots. Keep the tape taut to prevent wrinkles and press it down firmly. On wide stripes, there's no need to mask off the whole stripe – just the side edges.

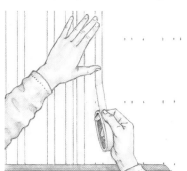

5 Applying the paint Following your design, carefully sponge your first paint colour on to all the unmasked stripes to be painted in this shade, taking the paint just over the tape edges. Clean the sponge thoroughly then use it to apply the second colour to the remaining unmasked stripes.

Use stripes of different widths and colours to build up attractive designs, like this elegant combination of mint green and lavender stripes. The stripes are sponged over a lavender-blue tinted white background in this sequence: 4cm (1½in) wide mint stripe, 2.5cm (1in) space, 8cm (3in) wide lavender stripe, 2.5cm (1in) space, 4cm (1½in) wide mint stripe, 6cm (2¼in) space.

6 Removing the tape When the paint is touch-dry, gently but steadily pull away the tape. If any of the base coat starts peeling away with it, stop and use a craft knife to slit along the edge of the lifting paint to release it and stop it lifting all along the stripe. Continue removing the tape. Touch up any areas where the paint has lifted with a small paint brush. Leave the wall to dry thoroughly. Brush off any chalk marks.

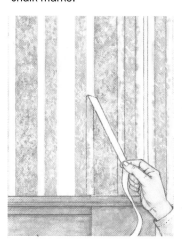

Painting stripes on to your wall, rather than using a wallpaper, gives you the freedom to create any design you like – and at a fraction of the cost of paper. Here are some ideas to inspire you.

▶ *A lounge with a seashore theme is set off perfectly by watery blue waves rippling across white walls. To copy this look, chalk a guideline on to the wall to indicate the centre of each wave; then paint a wavy line along each guideline, using a brush the desired width of the wave. Stop the waves at dado height so the effect isn't too overpowering.*

◢ *Wide stripes in bold primaries over a white background create a playful, circus-like atmosphere in a child's bedroom. For a textured finish, the stripes are applied using a lightly coated paint roller.*

◣ *Add a striking, contemporary look to your bathroom with evenly spaced stripes painted in vivid blue or another bright colour over a fresh white background. Choose accessories to match for a coordinated finish, and soften the effect with vases of fresh flowers.*

OIL GLAZE WORK

Oil glaze work, also known as scumble glazing, creates a softened broken-colour finish on walls and furniture. The effect enriches the surfaces, giving them depth, movement and texture.

Working with oil glazes may sound technical, but the process is really quite straightforward and the richness of the results definitely speaks for itself. Oil or scumble glaze is simply a transparent medium which you tint to the required shade with artists' oil colours. When applied over an oil-based basecoat, such as eggshell paint, the glaze spreads a soft, cloudy veil of colour over the underlying paint, creating a depth, movement and character not achievable with broken-colour effects worked with opaque paints.

By varying the application of the techniques and the colours and the surfaces on which you are working very different styles are created. These can range from a distressed, rustic style to a richer, sophisticated town house look. You can apply the techniques to both old and new walls and woodwork – the effects look different but equally good. Imperfections on older and roughened surfaces give a more textured, country farmhouse look, whereas when the technique is applied to smooth surfaces, a richer, smarter look is introduced into a room setting.

A vibrant viridian green glaze brushed over a buttermilk basecoat on the walls of this bathroom creates an evocative backdrop, reminiscent of the gently rippling surface of the sea.

OIL-GLAZING TECHNIQUES

The technique involves applying the glaze over the basecoat with a brush, then working over the wet glaze with either a brush or a cloth. Very different effects are achieved depending on how you work the glaze and what you use to work it. As a general guideline, a cloth creates a rough, natural texture, while a brush can give a very controlled, neat finish.

A popular way of finishing the glaze with a brush is to use a stippling technique. This gives a subtle, fine texture that is particularly suited to smaller areas or items, such as the skirting and architrave in a room or on furniture. The process involves using a dry, decorators' softening brush in a dabbing motion over the wet glaze. More information about stippling is given overleaf.

MIXING COLOURS

The best effects are created by applying the tinted glaze over a white or pale base coat. To tint a glaze, you can mix any number of artists' oil colours in varying amounts to achieve your desired shade. To create a feeling of depth you can apply two tinted glazes in different colours over the base coat. You can closely link the colours of the glazes, using, for example, a light shade followed by a darker, harmonious shade, or for a more dramatic effect you can use contrasting colour glazes, such as a blue over yellow. It is always advisable to experiment on a spare piece of board before starting a project, to make sure you like the effect your chosen colour combination produces.

When painting walls, it's important to mix sufficient coloured glaze to cover the desired area, as you will find it difficult to re-mix and obtain the same colour later. As a guide, two litres of mixed, coloured glaze covers a room measuring 4.5m (15ft) square with ease. It is a good idea to work on one wall at a time, as this allows enough time for you to perfect the finish before the glaze dries.

This effect is created with two toning green glazes over a white basecoat. Mix the tints for the glazes using artists' oil colours as follows: for the bright green glaze, mix 3 parts emerald green, 3 parts bright green and 1 part raw umber with a little white (mineral) spirit; for the dark green glaze, mix 3 parts terre vert, 2 parts viridian, 1 part raw umber, 1 part Paynes grey with a little white (mineral) spirit. Add to the prepared oil glaze in the ratio 1 part colour to 8 parts oil glaze medium.

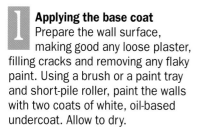

1 Applying the base coat
Prepare the wall surface, making good any loose plaster, filling cracks and removing any flaky paint. Using a brush or a paint tray and short-pile roller, paint the walls with two coats of white, oil-based undercoat. Allow to dry.

2 Mixing the oil glaze medium
Mix equal parts of oil-based glaze and white (mineral) spirit in the paint kettle. Stir thoroughly.

3 Mixing the first glaze In a paint kettle or tray, mix together artists' oil paints and a little white (mineral) spirit to the desired shade. Use a knife to mix this to a smooth, thick consistency.

4 Adding the oil glaze medium Using a clean paint tray or other suitable container, measure and pour in one part ready-mixed colour followed by eight parts oil glaze medium and mix well. At this stage the consistency should be like thin cream.

5 Applying the first glaze With a large, standard decorators' paint brush, roughly brush the tinted glaze over the wall in broad random strokes, crossing over your previous brush marks and leaving small spaces to show the white base coat.

6 Softening the brush marks Quickly pass a clean, dry softening brush (or cloth) over the glaze, blurring the brush marks and softly pushing the glaze over the small, unglazed spaces. Aim to create areas of darker and lighter tones. Allow to dry for 24 hours.

7 Mixing the second glaze Following steps 3 and 4, use darker shades of artists' oil paint to create a second tinted glaze.

8 **Applying the second glaze** Apply the second glaze as in step 5, but in this case leave slightly larger spaces between the brush strokes, to expose softened areas of the lighter glaze. Soften the effect as in step 6, to create a subtle, mottled effect in varying tones.

9 **Protecting the finish** To protect and enhance the oil glaze work, when the coloured glaze is thoroughly dry, apply two coats of clear varnish, allowing each one to dry between applications. A matt varnish gives a natural look, whereas a satin finish gives a sheen.

TIP

GLAZE RATIOS

For the best effects, mix the coloured glazes in the following ratios:

Walls: when mixing a glaze for walls, mix the tinted glaze in a ratio of 1 part ready-mixed colour to 8 parts prepared oil glaze medium.

Wood: when mixing glaze to stipple on woodwork and furniture, mix the tinted glaze in a ratio of 1 part ready-mixed colour to 3 parts prepared oil glaze medium.

STIPPLE-GLAZED TRAY

A stippled effect is a hardwearing finish to use on wooden kitchen accessories. To paint a wooden tray in the same way as the one shown here, as well as the materials listed on the previous page, you need a 2.5-5cm (1-2in) household paint brush. To copy the colour effect, mix the first glaze using 6 parts white, 2 parts Prussian blue, 2 parts raw umber and 1 part yellow ochre artists' oil paint and adding oil glaze medium. Make the second glaze by adding oil glaze medium to permanent blue artists' oil paint.

Choose colours from soft furnishings to decorate your accessories – this tray is stipple-glazed to match the table cloth.

1 Preparing the wooden tray Prepare the surface, then paint both sides with white oil-based undercoat, allowing the paint on one side to dry before painting the other. When dry, work the different stages of the glazed effect given below in the same way, on one side of the tray at a time.

2 Applying the first glaze Mix up the glazes as in *Oil-glazing Techniques*, steps 2-4, but in a ratio of 1 part colour to 3 parts oil glaze. Using a household paint brush, apply the first glaze sparingly, following the direction of the wood grain.

3 Stippling the glaze While the glaze is still wet, take a dry, clean, hog hair softening brush and dab this quickly in and out of the glaze. Continue until all the brush marks have disappeared and there are tiny soft dotted marks over the whole surface. Allow to dry thoroughly.

4 Applying the second glaze Apply the second glaze as the first. Using a dry, clean hog hair softening brush, stipple away brush marks so the glaze blends with the underlying colour. Stipple more heavily in some areas to create a shaded effect. Allow to dry.

5 Protecting the surface Paint two coats of matt or satin varnish over the glazed tray, allowing each one to dry thoroughly.

RAGGING

Ragging is a broken colour technique which creates a random pattern that echoes crushed velvet. This quick and easy paint effect is ideal for walls or fitted furniture such as a run of cupboards.

It's easy to get a pleasing result with ragging – a quick paint technique which uses rags to make patterns in thinned paint. The random pattern is perfect for adding interest to a large expanse of wall and is useful for disguising uneven or blemished surfaces. You can also use it when you want an interesting finish on smaller areas such as kitchen units, skirting boards and shelves.

Ragging requires very little equipment. All you need is two colours of a paint suitable for the surface, a roller, a paint brush and plenty of clean rags. Emulsion (latex) is usually the best choice of paint for a large area such as a wall. The technique can be used to produce a wide range of effects depending on the colours you choose, the sort of rag you use and how tightly you gather it up.

Ragging can be subtle or intense depending on your choice of colours. Here a sunny yellow ragged over white produces a cheerful result in a kitchen.

Ragging Techniques

There are three methods of ragging: ragging off, ragging on and rag rolling. Whichever method you choose, one or two coats of a base colour must be applied first and allowed to dry. When ragging, the pattern is affected by the way the rag is scrunched. The tighter the rag, the more dense the pattern will be. It's important to keep to the same degree of scrunching over a whole wall to avoid a patchy effect.

Ragging off is the most commonly used method. After allowing the base coat to dry, paint on a coat of thinned emulsion (latex) in a second colour. Scrunch up a rag and press it on to the wet painted surface to make a random pattern by removing some of the thinned paint to reveal patches of the base colour.

Ragging on produces a more pronounced pattern than ragging off. Once the base coat is dry simply scrunch up a dry rag and use it to apply the thinned emulsion (latex) in a second colour.

Rag rolling produces a more regular pattern than other methods. It should be done in vertical lines to produce an even effect. The thinned emulsion is first applied over the dried base coat as for ragging off. Then the rag is bunched into a sausage shape and lightly rolled up the wall in one movement to form a mottled strip. This rolling is repeated over the wall.

Choosing Colours

When planning your colour scheme, bear in mind that the best results are usually created by using a light shade for the base colour and ragging or rag rolling a darker shade over the top. Before you begin to paint a wall, buy some tester pots of paint and experiment with different colours on a sheet of lining paper. Stick the lining paper up on the wall with masking tape to check the result in natural and artificial light.

The safest way to achieve a successful result is to combine two tones of one colour; try peach ragged over pale apricot for a warm look or use a strong blue over a paler blue for a cooler effect. Avoid colours which are very close in tone or next to each other on the shade card, as these may be too similar for the effect to show up.

By experimenting with colour combinations you can create different effects. Pale grey or blue looks good over white for a pastel colour scheme; apricot over cream will have more of a cosy feel. Lime green over lemon yellow will produce a vibrant scheme. To create really dramatic effects choose strong colours such as wine or a fresh green over white or ivory.

Choosing Rags

Unglazed cotton is the traditional material for ragging, and old cotton sheets are perfect. For a softer effect you could also try cheesecloth, or a roll of decorator's cloth. Synthetic fabrics such as polyester are not suitable because they don't absorb the paint. Fabrics with a small amount of synthetic fibres such as a cotton/polyester blend would still work, but with less definition than pure cotton.

Experiment with different fabrics scrunched up tightly or held more loosely until you get the effect you want. Make sure you have a plentiful supply of cloths as the rags soon become clogged with paint – an ideal size is about 20 x 30cm (8 x 12in). Cut the cloth up into useable sizes before you start ragging – you must work quickly, particularly with the ragging off technique.

◨ *Deep peach emulsion was ragged over a very pale peach base coat, leaving a pattern and revealing areas of pale colour underneath.*

Ragging a Wall

Before painting, first carefully prepare the walls by filling any cracks and holes and sanding rough areas where necessary. The instructions opposite are for ragging off, but you can experiment with the variations of ragging on or rag rolling – see the instructions under Ragging Techniques above.

With ragging, the paint needs to be worked before it dries. If you are working by yourself, it is best to apply the thinned paint to one section of the wall at a time, then rag over it before moving on to the next section. If you can get a friend to help, one person can work ahead, applying the thinned paint, and the other can follow behind with the rag, removing some of the wet paint.

1 Applying the base coat Using a roller, apply a coat of the base colour. When this is dry, if necessary paint on a second coat. Allow to dry thoroughly before starting the ragging process.

3 Ragging off Scrunch up a rag and dab it lightly and quickly on to the wall, removing some of the thinned paint. Vary the direction of your hand and adjust the rag occasionally for a random pattern.

2 Applying the top coat In a paint kettle, gradually add water to emulsion (latex) paint in your second colour until the paint is thinner than the consistency of single cream. Brush the thinned paint over the base coat, working quickly over one section of the wall at a time.

4 Checking the effect Continue working over the wall, one section at a time. Stand back from the wall at intervals to check the result, and lightly touch in any missed areas. When the rag becomes clogged with paint, use a fresh rag or rinse it with water and squeeze out the excess before continuing.

Ragging Cupboard Doors

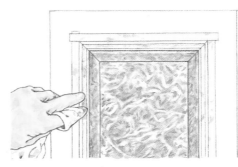
These kitchen units have been given a fresh coat of grey-green paint. The decorative detail is brought out by ragging inside the panels and using a brush stroke technique elsewhere.

Before you start on a large expanse of wall, you may prefer to experiment with a smaller ragging project such as wooden cupboard doors or kitchen units – the technique is just as successful over wood as over walls. The method is the same except that a tougher water-based or solvent-based satin finish paint is used instead of emulsion.

Ragging looks effective when used together with another paint technique. The cupboard door and drawer panels illustrated here have been ragged while the rest of the unit has been given a different finish, achieved by slowly and firmly dragging a paint brush over the surface in one direction so that the brush strokes are clearly visible.

All cupboards and units should be well cleaned before painting. Remove handles, then wash down doors and frames with hot soapy water. When dry, wipe over with methylated spirit (denatured alcohol).

YOU WILL NEED

❖ RUBBER GLOVES
❖ 5cm (2in) PAINT BRUSH
❖ WOOD PRIMER
❖ SATIN FINISH PAINT
❖ MASKING TAPE
❖ PAINT KETTLE
❖ WHITE (MINERAL) SPIRIT or WATER
❖ RAGS

1 Painting the base
Apply a coat of primer on new or bare wood. When dry, paint on a coat of satin finish paint in the base colour. Allow to dry. Mask off the area around the panels.

2 Applying the paint
Thin paint in the second colour with water or white (mineral) spirit (depending on if it's water- or solvent/oil-based), just thinner than single cream. Use paint brush to apply even coat to one panel.

3 Ragging the surface Scrunch up a clean dry cloth to the required tightness and dab it on to the thinned wet paint to leave a ragged pattern.

4 Picking out the moulding
Wrap your index finger in a clean piece of cloth and run it carefully around the moulded part of the door, to remove any thinned paint. Apply paint and rag off other panels in the same way. Leave to dry.

5 Painting panel surround (optional) Remove all masking tape. Apply a coat of thinned paint to areas around the panel and then draw a clean, dry brush slowly and firmly over the surface in one direction, leaving brush marks. Let paint dry.

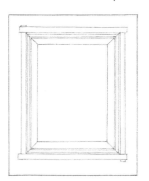

DRAGGING

Dragging is a subtle paint technique that can give a new lease of life to an inexpensive piece of old furniture and add a unique decorative finish to the walls and woodwork in your home.

D ragging is a traditional decorative paint finish similar to woodgraining. To achieve the attractive streaky effect you apply a semi-transparent glaze over a different base colour. Then you pull or drag a dry brush across the wet glaze so that some of it is removed to reveal thin lines of the base colour underneath.

In the eighteenth and nineteenth centuries, dragging was a popular way of making simple wooden furniture look more like the elaborate mahogany wardrobes and sideboards in grander homes. Interior designers no longer try to make dragging look like fake wood grain. Instead, it is used to add rich layers of colour and interesting surface texture to walls, doors and window frames, as well as furniture.

Different colour combinations create different moods – a pastel glaze over a white ground looks fresh in a bedroom or bathroom, whereas light and dark shades of a warm colour such as terracotta give a living room a welcoming glow.

The following pages show how to drag a wall, and how to drag a plain wooden box in an attractive striped design.

Walls dragged with a bright blue glaze over a pale blue base coat create an elegant backdrop for blue and white furnishings in this living room.

DRAGGING A WALL

You'll find it much easier to drag a wall if you have a helper. One of you can apply the glaze in bands about 60cm (2ft) wide, and the other can follow on behind to drag it. Keep the glaze well brushed out so that it doesn't run, and try to drag from the top to the bottom of the wall in one motion, so that the vertical stripes are continuous. If you cannot drag down the wall in one go, stop and restart the dragging fairly low down where the 'join' won't be so noticeable. Do not stop and start at the same place each time.

The steps below explain the technique for dragging using an eggshell base coat and an oil-based glaze. If you want to use water-based paints, mix and tint the glaze according to the manufacturer's instructions and follow the same steps.

PAINTS

You can either use oil- or solvent-based paints or water-based paints for dragging. The only thing you must not do is mix the two different types of paint, as they are incompatible. Most professional decorators use solvent-based paints because they are slow-drying and produce a more clearly defined dragged effect than water-based paints.

Choose eggshell paint for the background colour and an oil-based glaze (sometimes called a *scumble glaze*) for the top coat. Oil-based glaze is available from specialist decorating shops. It is fairly thick and creamy yellow in colour but dries to a transparent finish. Thin it down with an equal amount of white (mineral) spirit, and colour it with eggshell paint or artist's oil paints.

If you prefer to use water-based paints, use emulsion (latex) paint for the background colour and an acrylic scumble glaze for the top coat. Thin the glaze according to the manufacturer's instructions and tint it to the colour you want with either gouache paint, acrylic paint or a water-based tinting colour.

Whichever type of paint you choose, experiment with the colours on scrap paper until you are happy with the effect.

BRUSHES

The base coat and the glaze are both applied with ordinary decorating brushes – choose a size that suits the area you are working on. Use synthetic bristles for applying water-based paints.

Traditionally, the dragging is done with a dragging brush (sometimes called a 'flogger'). Dragging brushes have long, evenly spaced bristles and come in various sizes from 7.5cm (3in) to 15cm (6in) wide. They are expensive, but it's worth investing in a large one if you want to decorate a couple of rooms. A cheaper brush that is normally used for hanging wallpaper is also reasonably effective over a smaller area.

YOU WILL NEED

❖ PLASTIC SHEETING OR NEWSPAPER
❖ EGGSHELL PAINT
❖ OIL-BASED GLAZE
❖ WHITE (MINERAL) SPIRIT
❖ ARTISTS' OIL PAINT
❖ BUCKET (for mixing up glaze)
❖ DECORATING BRUSH
❖ DRAGGING BRUSH
❖ RAG to wipe brush
❖ POLYURETHANE VARNISH

1 Preparing the wall Make sure that the wall surface is smooth and even, and that it is clean and free from loose particles; rub over the wall with a clean duster if necessary.

2 Painting the base coat Apply the eggshell base coat with a decorating brush, and leave until completely dry.

3 Mixing the glaze Mix equal parts of glaze and white (mineral) spirit. Colour the glaze with artists' oil paint thinned with a little white (mineral) spirit. Pour paint into glaze gradually, and mix it in very well.

4 Applying the glaze Starting at one end of the wall, use a decorating brush to apply a smooth band of glaze, about 60cm (2ft) wide, over the base coat.

Dragging the glaze Work while the glaze is still wet. Hold the dragging brush so that the bristle tips just touch the glaze. Starting at the top of the wall, draw the brush firmly down the glaze with even pressure so that stripes of the base colour show through. Wipe the dragging brush with a rag now and then so that it stays dry. Repeat steps 4 and 5 until you have dragged the whole wall.

Varnishing Allow the glaze to dry completely. If you wish, you can finish the wall with one or two coats of varnish – this isn't essential, but gives the wall a more durable finish.

A yellowy-green glaze dragged over a white background gives this wall a fresh and tangy finish with an attractive texture. Avoid dragging rough, uneven walls, as the fine lines produced tend to highlight surface irregularities.

Filling cracks and dents

YOU WILL NEED

- ❖ FILLING KNIFE
- ❖ OLD PAINT BRUSH
- ❖ FILLER
- ❖ FINE-GRADE ABRASIVE PAPER
- ❖ SANDING BLOCK
- ❖ SELF-ADHESIVE JOINT TAPE
- ❖ CARTRIDGE OF DECORATOR'S MASTIC
- ❖ CARTRIDGE GUN for mastic
- ❖ CRAFT KNIFE

Main surfaces

1 Preparing the surface Use the corner of a filling knife to open up very narrow cracks to give the filler something to hold on to. Blow or brush out any loose dust, and using an old paint brush, brush some water along the crack or into the hole to stop the filler drying out too quickly and cracking.

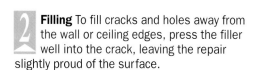

2 Filling To fill cracks and holes away from the wall or ceiling edges, press the filler well into the crack, leaving the repair slightly proud of the surface.

3 Sanding down When the filler has set hard, sand it down flush to the surrounding surface with abrasive paper wrapped around a sanding block.

Edge cracks

Use the materials described below rather than ordinary filler to repair cracks at the wall/ceiling join, at joins between sheets of plasterboard, or along the edges of skirting boards and door architraves. Ordinary filler will soon crack and fall out because of slight movement between the surfaces.

Filling joins

1 Using joint tape Rake out any loose material as above, then reinforce the angle between wall and ceiling, and any open joins between sheets of plasterboard, with self-adhesive joint tape.

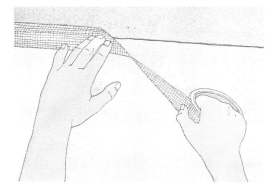

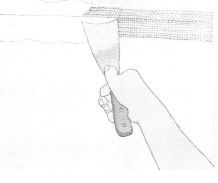

2 Concealing the tape Apply a skim of filler over the tape to conceal the open mesh. Paint over the filler when it has set, leaving a repair that won't crack again if movement re-occurs.

Filling gaps

1 Using a cartridge gun Place cartridge in gun with tip of nozzle cut. Squeeze trigger to force the mastic out. Press metal plate at back of gun to stop the mastic.

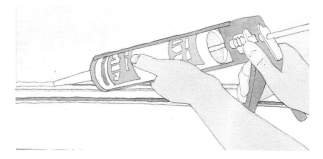

2 Using decorator's mastic Pipe the mastic between the wall and skirting boards or door architrave. Smooth it off neatly with a moistened finger. The mastic forms a surface skin which can be painted but which remains flexible, so preventing further cracks.

TIP

THE RIGHT CUT

Make the cartridge gun easier to use by cutting the tip of the nozzle off at an angle with a sharp craft knife – the further along the nozzle you make the cut, the larger the bead of mastic. For storage, push the cut off tip into the nozzle the other way round.

Painting: order of work

Working in a logical order saves time and effort, and gives a better result.

Woodwork around the home is subject to considerable wear and tear, and may well look as if it needs repainting before other surfaces require redecorating. Once your surface is well prepared, plan your order of work so that you are always working out from an edge that is still wet. For many wooden surfaces you may prefer to use varnish – the same rules apply.

If you're painting windows, or an external door, and don't want to leave them open overnight, start early in the morning and try to choose a fine, dry day. The room where you're painting must be well ventilated, so keep the windows and door open as much as possible.

Before you begin painting the walls or ceiling of a room, move all the furniture and ornaments out. If this is impractical, either position them in the middle of the room if there's enough space, or against one wall. You may have to paint one half of the room first, then move the furniture before you can do the other half, so think about the most logical place to put the furniture to save yourself moving it more than is absolutely necessary. If you do have to keep it inside the room you're painting, use plenty of dustsheets to protect it.

Order within a room

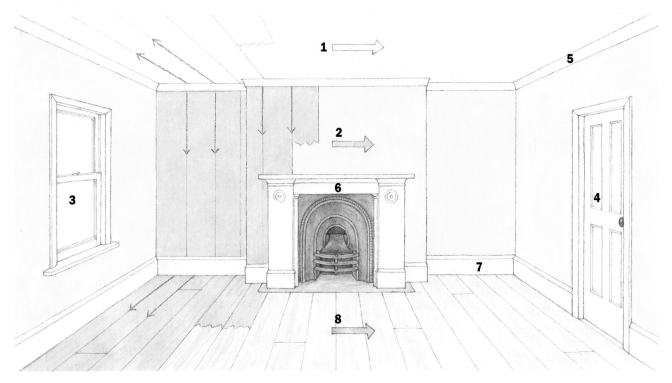

The illustration above charts the sequence of events when you are painting the entire room. Start by painting the ceiling, followed by the walls; in both cases work in overlapping bands, blending in the edges carefully. Paint away from the main source of natural light so that you can see clearly the area you've just painted.

Move on to the windows and doors (see overleaf). Next, paint any plasterwork details such as cornices or mouldings. Then tackle the fireplace, and finally the skirting boards and floor. Roll the carpet back from the skirting if possible. If not, use wide masking tape and a paint guard to protect the carpet as you work.

When you're not painting the whole room, simply follow the order given for the areas you do want to paint. Even when painting the individual elements in a room, follow the correct order of work to get the best finish.

Painting a staircase

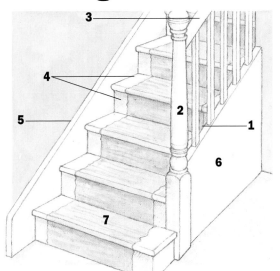

Work from the top down on each section, following the order shown. If you are laying a stair carpet, just paint the areas that will be exposed, but extend the paint to go at least 5cm (2in) under the carpet on each side.

37

Painting windows

Casement windows

Remove fittings if convenient. Protect the glass by stretching masking tape along the edge of the panes, but allow a gap of about 1.5mm (¹⁄₁₆in) between tape and wood so that the paint helps to seal the pane.

Have the opening casements wide open while you work, and follow the sequence in the diagram. Make sure that you paint any outside edges, too.

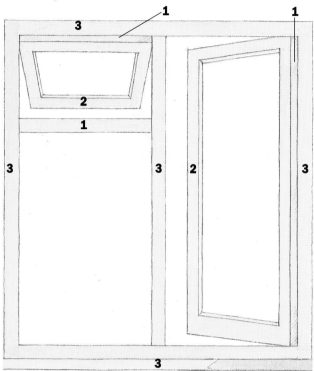

Sash windows

Protect the glass as described above. Then slide the top and bottom sashes up and down to expose different areas. Follow the sequence in the diagrams, taking care not to paint the sash cords.

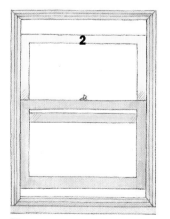

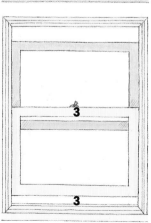

Key

 area to paint next

 area already painted

area of old paint

Painting doors

Panelled doors

Start by removing all the door furniture and wedging the door open. Following the sequence shown in the diagram, work quickly to avoid join marks between sections. Finish each section with brush strokes along the grain of the wood – this means you have to use both vertical and horizontal strokes on a panelled door. At the end, remember to paint the rim of the door to match the room it opens into so that it blends with the decor.

Flush doors

Flush doors should be painted in one session, from top to bottom. Work quickly so that the edges stay wet. Keep your strokes long and light, and don't overbrush. Brush in from the edges, never towards them, or the paint will build up, run, and a ridge will form.

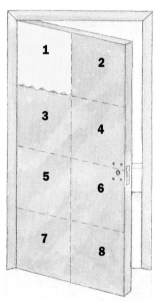

PAINTING IN TWO COLOURS

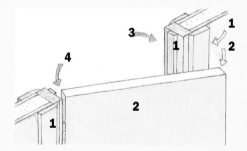

If you are painting your door different colours on either side, do the opening side first.

Paint the architrave and door frame up to and including the edge of the door stop (1) in your first colour. Then paint the face of the door and its opening edge (2) in the same colour.

Take your second colour and move to the opposite side of the door. Paint the architrave and frame up to and over the door stop (3). Finally, paint the opposite face of the door and its hinged edge (4) in the second colour.

Painting techniques

Find out how to apply paint to a surface correctly – the essential skill in getting the best result.

The technique you use for painting depends on three things:
- ❖ the tool you are using – brush, roller or pad.
- ❖ the type of paint you are using – in particular, how quickly it dries.
- ❖ the surface you are painting – its area and texture.

In many painting tasks you need to keep what professional decorators term a wet edge. As implied, it is the edge of the area you have just painted where the paint is still wet. This edge is used as the starting point for the next block of painting, so that the two areas blend inconspicuously. If the edge is allowed to dry, a visible, hardened ridge forms on the surface.

Before starting any painting job, buy at least enough paint to complete the first coat and make sure that all other surfaces within splashing range are protected by dust sheets or newspaper. Keep a clean rag and some brush cleaner handy in case of spills. Work in a clean room, in good light, from a safe, comfortable position.

Painting with a brush

A natural bristle brush is the traditional way of putting on gloss paint. For the main areas, use the largest size you feel comfortable with – say 50mm (2in) – but have a smaller one ready for the fiddly bits.

1 Using a new brush for the first time Before loading a new brush with paint, make sure you remove any loose or broken bristles by flicking it across your hand as though painting your palm.

2 Loading with paint Stir the paint (unless it is non-drip) and pour a little into a separate container. Dip the brush into the paint to cover the top third of the bristles and wipe off surplus on the edge of the container.

3 Brushing on the paint Holding the metal ferrule between your fingers and thumb, apply the paint over a small area of the surface in two or three vertical strips about 2.5cm (1in) apart. Brush across these at right angles to spread the paint evenly.

4 Laying off the paint Without re-loading the brush, finish off by painting light vertical strokes, brushing from the wet edge into the painted area so that you leave a thinner layer of paint along the sides. This is called laying off.

Using a brush for emulsion (latex) paint.
Water-based emulsion paints dry more quickly than gloss paints, so you need to modify your painting technique. Paint round any edges with a small brush before starting on the main body of the wall or ceiling. For the main areas use a much larger brush and hold it in the palm of your hand rather than between your fingers. Apply the paint as quickly as possible, working in two directions and feathering the wet edges by brushing the paint away to nothing.

Painting along an edge
Lay the paint brush on its side, so the bristles follow a straight line – known as 'cutting in'. A special brush with angled bristles is available for painting very thin sections, such as window glazing bars.

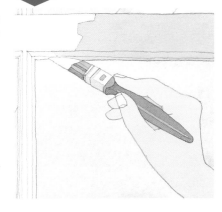

Using a roller

When it comes to painting walls and ceilings, most people choose to apply emulsion (latex) paint with a roller. You can't use a roller along edges, however, so you need to use a small paint brush to paint them before you start on the main expanse of wall or ceiling.

Be careful not to overload the roller to avoid spattering the area with excess paint.

Using a roller for gloss paint
Use a short-pile mohair roller for gloss paint; it is quicker than a brush, but not as quick as a pad, and it does tend to leave a slightly textured surface. Other types of roller are not suitable.

1 Using a roller for the first time Rinse a new roller thoroughly under the tap before using it, to make sure that you get rid of any loose bits of pile and dirt.

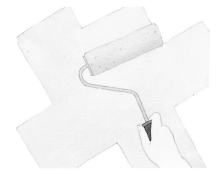

2 Loading the roller Load the roller by rolling it into a small amount of paint in the roller tray. Run the roller up and down the sloping surface of the tray to make sure that the paint is evenly spread throughout the pile. This ensures it does not drip.

3 Applying the paint Put the paint on the wall by drawing out a W or X shape. Then pass the roller across both horizontally and vertically so that the paint is spread evenly. On rough surfaces, be sure to work the paint into all the hollows.

Using a paint pad

A paint pad is ideal for putting on gloss paint, as it can spread paint more evenly than a paint brush. For flat areas, use the largest size you can comfortably hold; use a smaller pad on the mouldings of a panel door or the glazing bars of a window.

Using a paint pad for emulsion

(latex): Large pads, which are often fitted with extension handles, are used for walls and ceilings. The technique is similar to using a smaller paint pad for gloss paint – apply the paint in long smooth strokes until the pad is empty. Because the paint goes on more thinly than with a brush or a roller, you may need an extra coat, especially if you are covering a dark colour with a lighter one. Use a scrubbing action on rough or textured surfaces to work the paint into hollows.

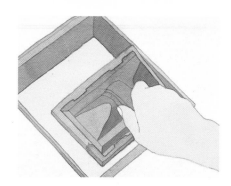

1 Using a new pad for the first time To avoid the tiny mohair bristles falling out, give a new pad a good clean in soapy water and then let it dry. Rub your hand roughly across the surface to make sure there are no loose bristles.

2 Loading with paint Partially fill the special paint pad tray with paint. Make sure that only the bristles are allowed to touch the paint – do not allow any paint to get into the foam backing – and wipe off excess paint on the side of the tray.

3 Applying the paint Paint the surface in adjacent vertical strips, the width of the paint pad, until it runs out of paint. Because the technique is so fast and the paint spreads very evenly, you don't need to worry about keeping a wet edge.

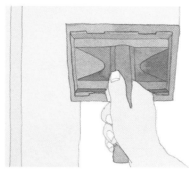

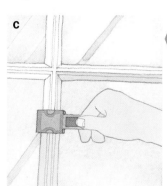

Painting an edge
There are speciality pads for awkward jobs:
(**A**) Some pads have wheels for painting right up to edges.
(**B**) Flexible pads are ideal for painting corners or edges.
(**C**) Small wands are handy for painting window frames.

Correcting faulty paintwork

Imperfections in the painted finish do happen, so it is worth knowing how to remedy them. Understanding the causes of painting faults also helps you to avoid them in the first place. Where the recommended remedy is to rub down and repaint, you should leave the surface to harden for at least a week before working on it.

Defect	Cause	Remedy
Runs, sags, tears	Paint applied too thickly or not laid off	Lay off if wet, otherwise allow to dry completely, rub down and repaint
Flaking	Poor surface preparation	Rub down, fill and repaint – or strip surface and start again
Blistering	Usually damp timber	Prick blisters to allow water to escape, rub down and repaint
Crazing (orange peel)	Incompatible paints	Rub down, fill and repaint or strip surface and start again
Wrinkles	Paint applied before previous coat has dried	Strip surface and start again
Grainy surface	Usually dust in the drying paint	Rub down and repaint
Brush marks	Poor quality brush, or insufficiently sanded surface underneath	Rub down thoroughly and repaint

RANDOM STENCILLING

*Break up a plain surface with scattered stencilled motifs
in two or more colours, or group them together to form larger
designs for extra impact.*

U sing a single stencil you can create a variety of original decorative effects on a wall. Unlike a stencil border that forms a continuous repeat pattern along a wall, a single stencil motif either stands on its own as a complete decoration or can be repeated at random as many times as you like, in as many places as you want, to create a pattern. With one little butterfly you can print a cloud of beautiful butterflies.

The motif may be a delicate spray of flowers, carefully positioned to highlight a feature such as an arch in a room, or a group of cheerful teddy bears to add colour and excitement to a corner in a child's bedroom. Single motifs printed all over the wall, and edged with a stencil border, look just as attractive as a wallpaper and its matching border, and cost half the price.

As with any type of stencil, you can pick out small details of the design and stencil them independently on to pieces of furniture and other accessories for a fully coordinated look to the entire room.

A sage-green bow and ribbon design provides an elegant heading for a dried flower wreath. For a design with a stronger impact, you could paint the flanking ribbons in another colour. Examples of mixed colour stencils follow.

MULTI-SHEET STENCILLING

Instead of masking off the areas of the design to be painted in different colours, multi-sheet stencilling calls for a separate cut stencil sheet for each colour. In order to position every colour accurately, you must line up each stencil sheet precisely on top of the part of the design that is already printed – this is known as the registration. Generally, it's best to print the lightest colour first and the darkest one last of all, so use the sheets in that order.

REGISTRATION METHODS

The registration method depends on whether the stencils are made from clear acetate or manila card. Read the registration instructions on the pack carefully before you start stencilling.

Acetate stencils are the easiest to use because they are transparent. The entire design is visible through the stencil sheets, even when you are colouring a different area of the design. Each stencil sheet usually has the outline of the rest of the colours in the motif printed on it so that it's easy to line them up with the sections of the design that you have already stencilled.

Card stencils have a V-shaped notch cut off the top and bottom edges, or holes pierced in the four corners. These are called *registration marks*. When the first stencil is in position, mark the notches or holes on the wall with a pencil. Line up the notches or holes on the subsequent stencil sheets with these marks for perfect registration.

POSITIONING THE MOTIF

To test the position of the stencil motif on the wall, stencil a piece of scrap paper first. Then cut out this paper motif and attach it to the wall with masking tape. Stand back to view the effect, and then reposition the paper design as many times as you like until you are satisfied with the result. Lightly mark the position for the stencil in a soft pencil on the wall by drawing round the test motif and remove the piece of paper.

YOU WILL NEED

❖ STENCILS

❖ STENCIL PAINTS AND BRUSHES

❖ MASKING TAPE OR SPRAY ADHESIVE

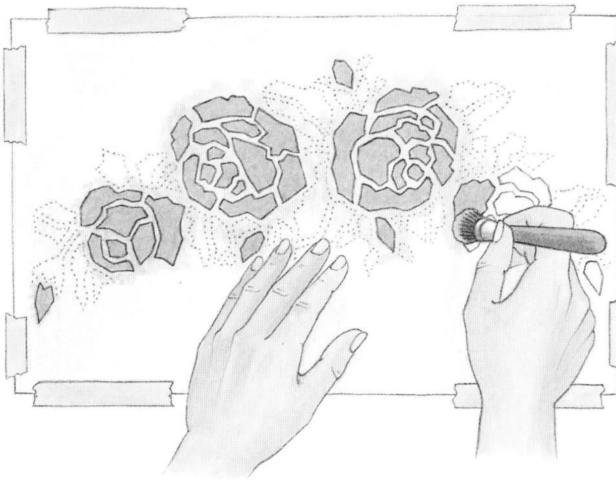

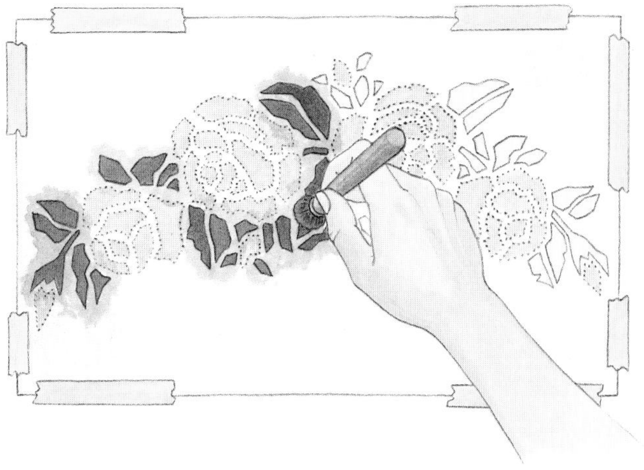

1 **Positioning the first stencil** Fix the stencil sheet for the first colour in position on the wall with masking tape or spray adhesive. Apply the paint with a light dabbing motion, and leave to dry. Carefully remove the stencil.

2 **Using the next stencil** Place the stencil for the second colour over the stencilled first colour. Check that the stencil is correctly registered, and secure in place as before. Apply the second colour and leave to dry.

3 **Printing further colours** Register and print any remaining colours in the same way. Always check that the paint is completely dry before printing another colour, otherwise the design may smudge.

▼ A large rose and leaf stencil frames a picture. The colours of the stencil echo the soft watercolours of the print.

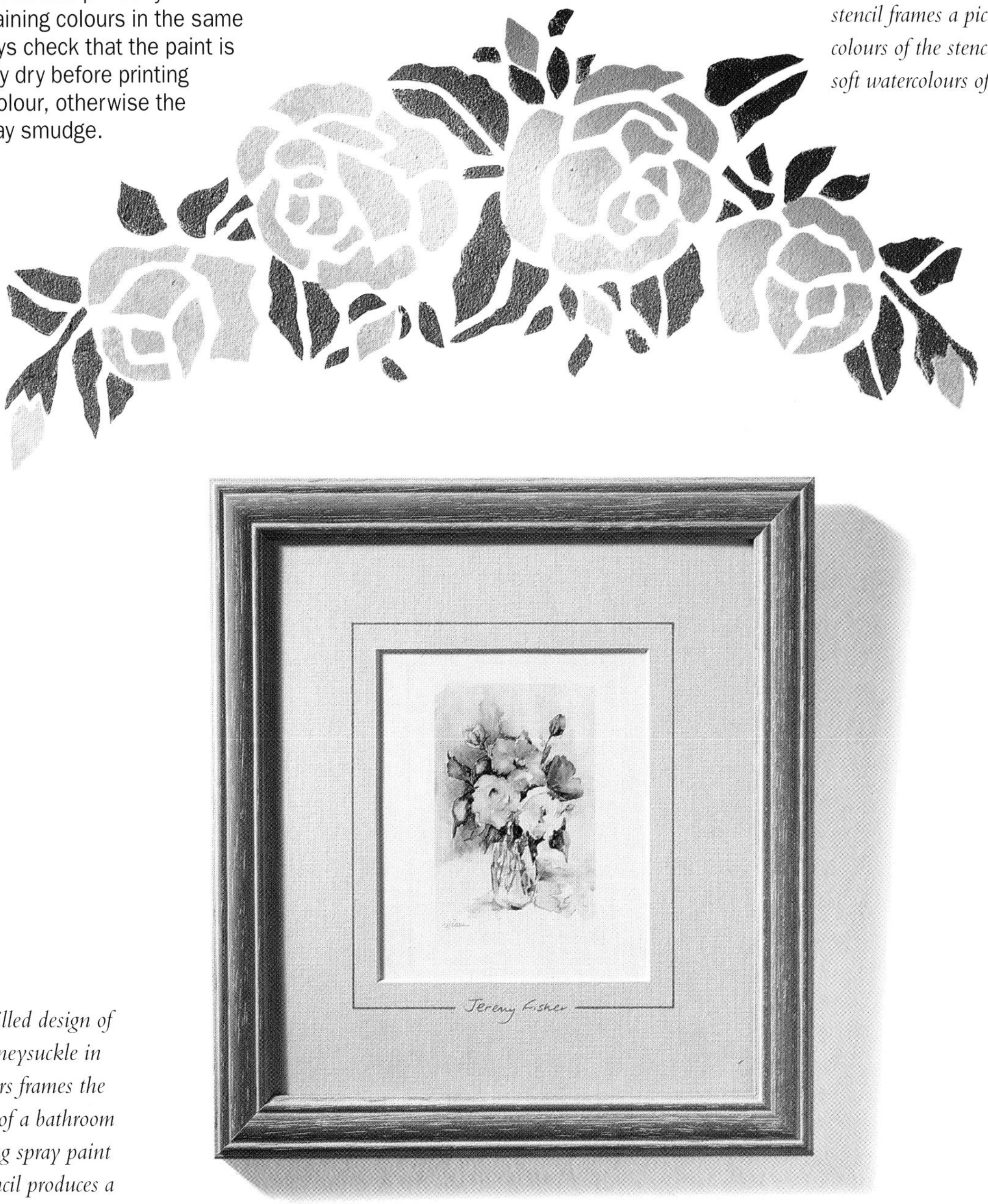

◄ A stencilled design of trailing honeysuckle in three colours frames the top corner of a bathroom shelf. Using spray paint for the stencil produces a soft, diffused look.

STENCILLED DETAILS

Stencilling works effectively on a wide range of wall surfaces, from plain painted walls, wallpaper and painted brickwork to wooden tongue-and-groove or dado panelling – it just depends on the decorative look you want.

Almost any room in your home gets a new lease of life from a stencilled design or two, arranged in formal patterns or apparently at random. Another advantage of a stencil is that it instantly personalizes anything it adorns.

A benefit of stencil designs is their complete flexibility. There is an almost limitless supply of motifs, and even if you don't find exactly what you want in kit form, you can always originate your own stencils or copy a design from a book or magazine. Stencilling works equally well in elegant formal surroundings, such as drawing rooms as in bright informal playrooms – you can be as subtle as you want, or as bold as you dare.

▲ *An abstract stencil design in soft red and green positioned on the panels of an internal door complements the ceramic door knob and door plate.*

▼ *A bedroom decorated in pretty blue and cream floral fabric looks even more romantic with the addition of bird and flower stencils positioned randomly on cream-washed walls.*

▲ *This elegant white fitted bedroom has a crisp clean look. The stencilled vase of flowers and the tulips either side add a stylish finishing touch.*

▶ *Stencils can be used in the most surprising places – here a heart-inspired floral motif draws attention to an attractive brass light fitting.*

Stencilling a Border

A stencilled room has a charm all of its own. Follow this simple guide to stencilling attractive and effective borders, and enhance the look of your home.

As well as looking very appealing, a stencilled border can have an architectural impact, in the same way as a wallpaper border. It can highlight existing features such as arches and fireplaces, and make featureless interiors more interesting. In a room with bare walls, a stencilled border can add character and subtly alter the proportions of the room, making it look more elegant, or cosier.

A stencilled border can be used at skirting board, dado or picture rail level, or immediately below the ceiling to make it seem lower. Around windows and doors a stencilled border frames and decorates in the same way as a wallpaper border, but with a more individual character.

Also, of course, any part of a border stencil can be picked out and reproduced as a separate motif on items of furniture and accessories, for a coordinated room colour and pattern scheme.

A stencilled border can be continuous or non-continuous. A continuous border is a line of motifs repeated without any breaks. Usually the stencil is self-overlapping, and made from clear acetate so that you can easily register the overlaps.

A non-continuous border is a line of repeated but separate motifs and is made with a stand-alone stencil. The stencil can be made of acetate or card; acetate is often easier to use as it is flexible and transparent.

Stencilling a border isn't difficult if you use a pre-cut stencil. It's also worth paying a little extra for Proper stencil paint when stencilling a border; its quick drying properties allow you to work steadily around the room without having to keep stopping to wait for it to dry.

Real shells, coral and a sea sponge are a perfect complement to the marine theme of this stencilled bathroom wall. The pattern incorporates a border of shells, with the motifs neatly reversed.

PLANNING THE BORDER

Careful planning is the key to a successful stencilled border. First decide on the position of the border. If you put it immediately above or below a dado or picture rail, or at ceiling height or skirting board level, you have a ready line to guide you. Otherwise, use a level to find the true horizontal, and lightly pencil a dotted line all the way around the wall to mark the top or bottom of the stencil, as appropriate.

CONTINUOUS STENCILLING

With a continuous border, start by marking the mid point of the most eye-catching section of wall. Centre the first stencil above or below this mark as appropriate, then work away from it in both directions.

You can continue some designs straight around corners without a break – bend the stencil around the corner and hold it firmly in place while you apply the paint. With other designs it is best to stop when you reach a corner, then start again from the centre of the next section of wall. When this is the case, always lengthen rather than shorten the design if it doesn't fit into the

corner exactly – a shortened design always looks wrong. In all cases, because walls are rarely absolutely straight or corners at true angles, make slight adjustments by eye to keep the border on line.

When the design calls for more than one colour, a separate stencil for each colour is usually supplied, with only the relevant parts cut out on each, so there is no need for masking. Apply one colour at a time, working all the way around the room before starting with the next colour. Wait until you have finished the border and all the paint has dried before erasing pencil marks.

◪ *A continuous stencil such as this attractive pear border can be run vertically or horizontally.*

1 **Positioning the first stencil** Centre the first stencil at the mid point of the wall, aligning it with the horizontal, and secure all round the edges with small strips of tape. Apply the paint, and leave to dry.

2 **Continuing the design** Carefully peel the stencil off the wall, keeping the tape intact. Reposition the stencil so that the pattern overlaps exactly. Apply the paint as before. Continue along the wall, then repeat for each separate colour until the whole border design is complete.

HANGING DADO PANELS

By far the easiest way of hanging a solid embossed wallcovering such as Lincrusta is to use pre-trimmed dado panels below a border or rail. If you have an existing dado rail, buy panel lengths to fit the wall beneath. Otherwise, finish off the top edge by hanging a Lincrusta border or adding a moulded dado rail.

YOU WILL NEED
- ❖ TAPE MEASURE, PENCIL
- ❖ SPIRIT LEVEL, PLUMB LINE
- ❖ DADO PANELS
- ❖ SPONGE, soft CLOTHS
- ❖ PASTING TABLE, BRUSH
- ❖ LINCRUSTA GLUE OR VINYL-OVER-VINYL GLUE
- ❖ CRAFT KNIFE or SCISSORS

1 Measuring up If you have no dado rail, measure the length of the dado panel and use a spirit level to mark a horizontal line along the wall from which to hang the panels. Drop a plumb line to mark a vertical guideline for the first panel.

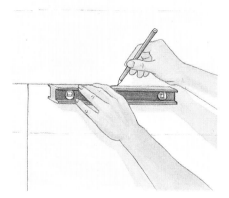

2 Soaking the backing Sponge the paper backing of each panel with warm water and leave them to soak, stacked flat back to back, for 20-30 minutes or as recommended by manufacturer. Wipe off surplus water with a dry cloth.

3 Applying glue Brush the Lincrusta or vinyl-over-vinyl glue on to the back of the first panel. If the glue is too thick to spread, stir vigorously but do not dilute. Make sure the whole surface, especially the edges, is evenly covered.

4 Hanging the panels Hang the first panel immediately you have applied the glue, aligning the top with your guideline or the dado rail and one edge with the vertical line. Smooth into position with a cloth pad, paying particular attention to edges – do not use a seam roller. Wipe off any surplus glue, and continue glueing and hanging panels.

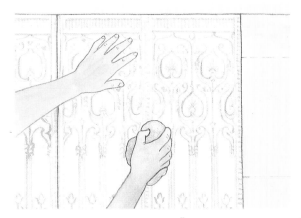

5 Turning corners If the corner is well rounded, ease the panel round the angle, making sure the seam does not fall near an outward angle. For a sharp corner, cut and hang the panel in two sections, butting the cut edges together at the corner – do not overlap. When you are cutting the panel, use a craft knife and angle the cut slightly for a mitred finish.

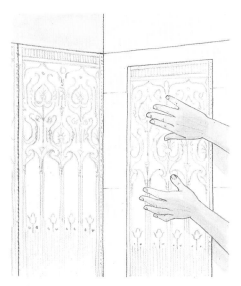

6 Finishing off Leave the panels to dry for at least a couple of days. If necessary, fill any imperfections at corners with a little putty. Allow to dry then prepare the surfaces for painting by wiping down the panels with a cloth dipped in white (mineral) spirit.

Painting Embossed Wallcoverings

Leave the wallcovering to dry out thoroughly before painting. Check through the details below to find the right type of paint for the wallcovering you are using. Either paint in the normal way, using a soft brush to work the paint well into the recesses, or try a simple paint technique to emphasize the raised pattern.

Medium/light embossed, blown vinyls Most water- or solvent/oil-based paints are suitable – depending on the finish you want, a matt or silk emulsion (flat or satin latex) or a solvent/oil-based satin or gloss paint all give a good result. Build up several coats of colour until you get the desired effect.

Heavy embossed For solid, oil-based wallcoverings like Lincrusta you must use a solvent/oil-based paint as a first coat – a water-based paint won't adhere. Use either an eggshell or a gloss finish. If you prefer a matt finish, use a solvent/oil-based paint under two or more coats of emulsion – bear in mind that this finish is not as durable as a completely solvent/oil-based system.

Special techniques Experiment with a simple paint technique to enhance the overall effect of the wallcovering. Brush on a base coat of the right type of paint for the wallcovering as described above and leave to dry. Working in sections, quickly brush on a tinted glaze, or a second colour of paint, then use a soft cloth to rub off some of the wet glaze or paint from the raised pattern to leave colour in the recesses. Leave to dry and repeat the process if you want a greater depth of colour.

▲ *Because an embossed wallcovering can be sealed with several coats of paint, it is suitable for all areas of the home, even a steamy bathroom. The rich colour on these walls is a perfect match for the blue floor tiles.*

◄ *To emphasize the emboss on this wall frieze, a tinted glaze was applied over a base coat and then wiped off the raised surfaces.*

▲ *To add character to your walls, experiment with different effects and colours on a spare piece of wallcovering. For the subtle blue finish, emulsion was lightly wiped on with a cloth, and then wiped off the emboss to reveal the white base coat. For the reddish effect, a tinted glaze was brushed over a pale base coat, and then wiped off the raised area.*

WORKING WITH WALLPAPER

*Use a wallcovering to transform a room with colour,
pattern and texture – it can also be the best solution for disguising
less than perfect walls.*

There's a huge range of wallcovering designs on the market – classics include florals, mini-prints and stripes. If you don't want to limit yourself to one design, try a combination of plain and patterned, or consider a coordinated range – many floral wallpapers are designed to team with a mini-print, with the two papers linked by colour or motif. The same pattern theme is often available in furnishing fabrics, giving lots of mix-and-match opportunities.

When choosing wallcovering, get a large sample or buy a single roll and pin some up in the room for a few days, to check the effect in both natural and artificial light. Buy all the wallpaper you need at the start, checking that the batch numbers are the same. Some stores allow you to return unopened rolls – check when you buy. An extra roll may be useful for making good any future worn areas. If you should find you've underestimated and are forced to buy more paper from a different batch, try to use the odd roll where it won't show. Always read the label on the roll before you start hanging a wallcovering as the method may vary.

A well-hung, traditional floral wallpaper, teamed with a toning plain wallpaper below the dado rail, gives a smart, decorative finish to a wall. The dado rail itself provides a guideline against which to fix a coordinating border.

HANGING WALLPAPER

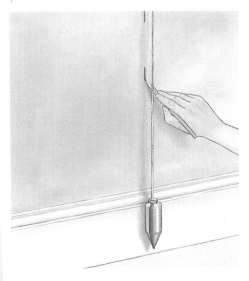

1 Marking a straight line To ensure the wallpaper hangs straight, suspend a plumbline to mark points on a vertical line against which the first drop will be hung.

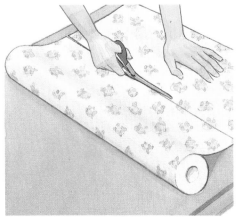

2 Cutting the drop Lay wallpaper face up on the pasting table and measure out the first length adding 15cm (6in) to allow for trimming at top and bottom. Make sure that a full pattern motif will be at the top of the wall where it is most obvious. Pencil in the cutting line, check that it is straight, then cut with long-bladed scissors.

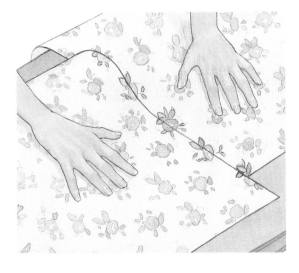

3 Matching the pattern Check the next length against the first one to match the pattern across the join. Pencil in the cutting line, then cut along it. From now on, measure up and cut all lengths as the first. Mark the top of each length to avoid hanging patterns upside-down.

4 Pasting Follow instructions on the paper for soak times. To paste paper, lay the first length face down, one side aligned with the table edge. Working quickly, paste from the centre outwards, spreading paste evenly right to the edges over half the length.

GETTING STARTED

FIXTURES AND FITTINGS

The clearer the walls the easier it is to paper them. Anything fixed to the walls with wallplugs is best removed. Push matchsticks into the wallplugs – they will stand out under the wallpaper as you hang it, to mark the position for rehanging the fittings.

PREPARING THE WALLS

The wall surfaces must be sound before you start wallpapering. Remove old wallpaper, make good any poor plaster and fill cracks. Sand down any repairs and lightly sand over all the walls before you paper.

SIZING THE WALLS

Seal new plaster with size – this is a watered down adhesive which seals the plaster and provides slip so the wallpaper slides easily into position. Leave at least an hour between sizing and papering.

THE FIRST DROP

Start alongside the largest window and plan to work away from the light, so that if any edges do overlap they will not cast a shadow and look obvious. Centre large-patterned papers on a focal point such as a chimney breast, then work outwards in both directions from that point.

5 Folding the paper Fold the pasted paper in half, pasted sides together. Move the folded section along so it hangs over table end; paste remaining paper. Fold the second half over, leaving a gap in the middle. To carry paper to wall, drape it over your arm.

TIP

HIDING THE JOIN

A wallpaper border not only adds a neat and attractive finish to your redecorated walls, it also helps disguise an untidy edge between wall and ceiling or skirting board.
There's a range of borders to suit most wallcoverings, and some manufacturers produce papers with coordinating borders.
Make sure you choose an adhesive that's specially made for the border of your choice.

6 Hanging the paper Using a stepladder to reach the top of the wall, unfold the upper half of the paper leaving the lower fold still in place. Overlap the top edge on to the ceiling or cornice by 8cm (3in) with a full pattern motif at the top. Slide wallpaper into position, aligning the edge with the vertical guideline on the wall.

7 Brushing on to the wall Use a paper-hanging brush or sponge to press paper against the wall – brush down the centre, then out to the edges. If the paper bubbles or wrinkles, gently peel it off to release air and brush it back into place – little bubbles often disappear as paper dries. Unfold lower half and brush it out in the same way.

8 Trimming the edges Press the top edge into the angle between the wall and ceiling with the back of a scissor blade. Peel back the paper, cut along the crease and use the tip of the hanging brush to dab the paper back into place. Trim the lower edge in the same way. Wipe off paste from the ceiling or woodwork and pasting table with a damp cloth or sponge.

9 Matching the pattern Paste and hang the next drop, matching the pattern exactly by sliding the paper up or down using the palms of your hands. Brush into place and trim as before. Gently run a seam roller over the join about 20 minutes after hanging. Don't roll embossed papers – dab the seams firmly with the hanging brush.

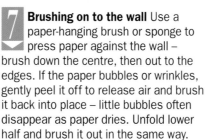

SPECIAL TECHNIQUES

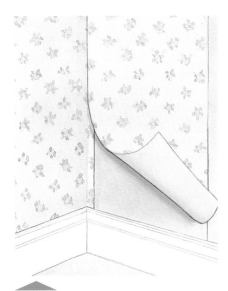

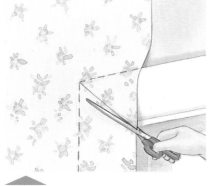

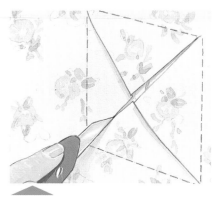

Turning a corner Hang paper that turns a corner as two strips. Measure the distance from the last drop to the corner. For internal corners, add 1.5cm (⅝in); for external corners add 3.5cm (1⅜in). Cut a length of paper to this width; hang it with the cut edge brushed into and around the corner. Measure the width of the rest of the paper then measure this distance from the corner. Hang a plumbline from this point and mark a vertical line. Hang the paper to this line, with your cut edge in the corner, overlapping the amount carried round from the adjoining wall.

Papering around doors and windows Hang the length in the normal way, but allow it to hang over the closed door. Make a diagonal cut into the corner. Trim paper roughly to the shape of the frame, allowing about 2.5cm (1in) overlap. Brush the paper into the angle between wall and frame, mark a crease line with the back of the scissors and trim.

Using lining paper Paper that is to be painted should be hung vertically as for standard wallpaper. If it is going under a wallcovering, hang it horizontally to avoid joins coinciding. Use the same paste that will be used for the final wallcovering. Start at the ceiling level and work down, butting joins closely. Leave to dry for 24 hours. Lightly sand down overlapping edges.

Papering around switches and sockets Paper straight over a switch or socket, using a sharp knife to make diagonal cuts to the corners (or several cuts if it is circular). Press the flaps back into position and trim the edges.

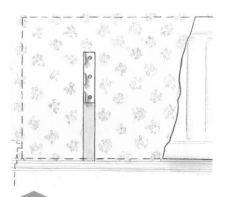

Papering around radiators Let the paper hang over the face of the radiator, and cut out a strip from the bottom of the length so that the paper can pass either side of the radiator bracket. Tuck paper behind radiator, smooth down as far as possible and trim. Check visibility of coverage along bottom, and patch from below if necessary.

Papering a window recess Paper the inside of the recess first, bringing a 5cm (2in) flap up on to the surrounding wall. Then paper the wall round the window, cutting round the shape of the window and pasting over the flap.

Once the electricity is switched off at the mains, some switches can be unscrewed from the wall and the wallpaper trimmed and tucked underneath for a really neat finish.

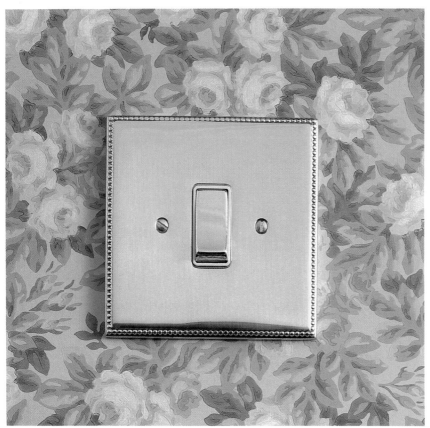

WALLPAPER PANELLING

Give your room a graceful eighteenth century air with elegant mock panelling cleverly created from lengths of wallcovering and framed with wallpaper border.

Wallpaper panels are a wonderful way of adding decoration to painted walls, and if you haven't wallpapered before, this is a perfect introduction. You just cut your chosen wallcovering into lengths , hang it as panels round the wall and then use a wallpaper border to frame each panel.

Try positioning a panel each side of a fireplace or hang them inside an alcove. Or use three panels to break up a large, featureless expanse of wall. Wallpaper panels also look good positioned above a dado rail, with the walls painted in different plain colours above and below.

You can make your panels from any patterned wallpaper. The panel design can be one single large pattern repeat, several smaller repeats or an all-over pattern such as a stripe. As you only need fairly small amounts to create a spectacular effect, you can go for more expensive wallpaper designs if these take your fancy.

Wallpaper borders can coordinate with the panel or you could create the impression of architectural moulding with a classical design such as a simple beading or rope effect or perhaps a traditional pattern. There's no need to hang lining paper under the panel – you can hang the panels straight on to plain painted walls.

Hang classical style wallpaper panels for a sophisticated look. Here, a single pattern repeat is exactly the right size for a panel.

IN THE FRAME

Rather than hang any old pictures just for the sake of having something on the wall, it is much more satisfying to seek out prints and paintings of subjects that interest you and group them together in an imaginative way.

The idea of grouping pictures on a wall according to a particular theme that interests you is very appealing. It immediately suggests that you want the group to be viewed as a whole, and together the pictures command more attention than if they were displayed in solitary splendour.

Animals and plants are particularly rich sources of picture material. Within the natural world there is something to suit all tastes from the cute and pretty to the wild and fantastic. Animal lovers can hunt down flocks of birds or shoals of fish to hang together on a wall, while plant fanciers can root round for herbaceous borders full of paintings, prints or engravings of fruits, flowers and leaves.

Since the very earliest cave paintings, artists and illustrators have interpreted the natural world in many different ways, producing everything from perfectly lifelike portraits to highly stylized and cartoon representations of wildlife. In your displays, you can either concentrate on the regularity and similarity of frames and images, or deliberately go for frames with different shapes and colours and diverse styles of artwork to create more eclectic groupings.

Groups of pictures have a way of growing, as you add more images to your arrangement. You can even create links between the pictures in a group with a stencilled design, cord or ribbon. However, don't let a group get too large, or it starts to look straggly.

Honours are evenly divided in this display between two birds, two fish and two farm animals. It's a very collectable group of colourful prints that could grow and grow.

◀ *The most successful picture groupings* have a definite pattern to their layout. Here, for example, different sizes and styles of floral studies are ranged very effectively round the head of a bed.

▲ *Making the frames*, rather than the images they encase, the focus of attention is an equally effective approach to arranging pictures. Here, the frames are many and varied, while the photocopied engravings of flowers and leaves are relatively low-key.

▲ *Perched symmetrically in place* above the fireplace, two bird prints reinforce the rich and slightly formal tones of the room. The choice of the strong brown mountboard for the prints acts as a balance to the deep timber of the mantelpiece below.

▶ *Plump peaches*, pears and apples, carefully depicted in rich red and golden tones, are in keeping with the understated elegance of this room. The wide, white mounts and bird's-eye maple frames set the prints off well against the pale walls.

SUSPENSE STORIES

Fine tune your picture collection by suspending each image with a series of pert bows, lengths of silken cord or swags of soft chiffon. The trim can be highly functional or purely decorative.

For a finishing flourish to a room, hang up your prints and pictures in an inventive way. The method you employ can be as simple as a grosgrain ribbon, twisted into a discreet bow and used to frame the picture, or as flamboyant as a drape of dreamy muslin, falling well below the base of the picture itself. It is a great way of linking a series of mismatched images, or making a simple print look more interesting.

On the whole the easiest way to achieve the effect is to hang up the picture in the conventional way, using a basic hook fixed to the wall behind. The device that you use to decorate it can then be more unexpected. There is no need, for instance, for a picture bow to take the weight of the picture – it can be suspended from a decorative hook positioned just above the picture and, if you allow the tails to hang below the picture, it will look like the main support.

If a picture bow can work in this way, why not try a less conventional means of support? A long silken scarf, for example, provides a fragile, softening touch as it slithers down the wall behind the picture. To add textural impact, try twisting ropes of decorator's cord or even raffia together in a number of strong colours.

A picture rail provides the obvious means of support for this symmetrical arrangement – yet the cord used to hang the picture is far from conventional. It becomes an important part of the total display and helps to link the composition.

95

▶ *Creamy grosgrain ribbon adds grace to these understated botanical prints. The ribbon, cut and stitched into a flat bow and suspended from a dainty picture hook, is strong enough to take the weight of the print. The brass picture hook is a clever touch, as it subtly echoes the glinting gold of the frame.*

◀ *The bold bow, in this case, is of prime importance to the overall image. It repeats the fabric used as a backing for the daffodil print and, courtesy of its large scale, it adds the missing element of drama to what would otherwise be a very simple image.*

▲ *Lengths of strong wire, looped over the top of the picture rail and attached to the back of each framed print, provide imaginative, but not intrusive, support.*

▶ *Swathes of muslin, suspended from gilded mouldings and linking the rows of pictures, add a softening touch to a formal display. The muslin is purely decorative – the pictures are supported by picture hooks.*

DISPLAYING PLATES

When it comes to adding instant interest to a bare stretch of wall, pretty plates, grouped together in clusters, displayed singly or hung in horizontal or vertical rows, are an innovative option.

H anging decorative plates makes a pleasant change from, or addition to, conventional paintings, prints or posters. It's also a more immediate and economical project – the chances are you already have some plates worth hanging. Porcelain, china, earthenware or glass, glazed or unglazed, highly decorated or plain – whatever looks right in the room is fine.

Souvenir plates are designed to be hung on walls but there's no need to stop there. Antique shops often have beautiful but reasonably priced plates with barely visible hairline cracks or chips which make them unsuitable for normal use but ideal for wall display. For fun on a budget, collect and hang antique saucers, since these often remain once their cups are broken and, again, are relatively inexpensive. And because they are small, you can display several in a modest space. If you can't run to genuine antiques, many manufacturers do excellent reproductions

Try to relate the display to furniture, such as above a sofa, or hang plates above a fireplace or door, on a narrow wall between two doors or windows or just under the ceiling, like a wall frieze.

Play safe with valuable plates – display them on plate stands on a shelf rather than hanging them from a wall. Clip-on wire holders are fine for plates that aren't too precious, but if you want to avoid scratching the plate use a special adhesive pad and ring stuck to the back of the plate.

A mixed medley of old-fashioned blue and white plates forms a flower-like focal point, reflecting the colour scheme of the bedlinen.

▲ **A single plate** topped by a coordinating bow adds cheer to any wall. Consider hanging a fun plate like this in a bathroom – unlike a poster or print, it won't be damaged by steamy conditions.

▲ **Enlivening a wall,** green glazed serving plates with Victorian-style sculptured motifs link the Victorian wall tiles and fruit bowl below with the row of green mugs above. The overall effect is one of quiet restraint, in keeping with the kitchen's simple decor.

◨ **Ribbon laced round** a filigree rim turns an inexpensive plate into an eye-catching wall display. A glass plate is ideal on patterned wallpaper like this, as the floral design shows through to enhance the effect.

◨ **A trio of plates** linked by a tasselled cord make a fine display. Plates don't have to match to work well together – these three came from diverse sources but they team up nicely as they share a botanical theme.

◀ **Panel design**
*To add a focal point to a plain
expanse of field tiles, consider a
picture panel such as this spring tulip
display. Choose from the same range
as your field tiles, or ensure all tiles
are the same size and thickness.*

◀ **Mosaic effect**
*Mosaic-style tiles in three shades of blue
conjure up images of the sea and break up a
large expanse of wall.*

▶ **Adding interest**
*Plain white tiles are enlivened with a border
frame and matching inset patterned tiles.*

Border tiles are useful for finishing off an
edge halfway up a wall or for dividing plain
and patterned tiling.

Full size border tiles, usually found in
mass produced ranges, have a border pattern
printed across the upper section and can be
used in the middle of a wall, to divide plain
and pattern, or at the top.

Narrow border tiles are the same width as
general purpose or decor tiles but about
76mm (3in) deep, and can be used to finish a
line of tiling, or to divide a large area. Relief
borders have raised decoration.

Dado tiles are a ceramic version of the
wooden dado rail and are usually found in
more expensive ranges. The tiles are always
plain, but sometimes embossed, and are used
to divide or top coordinated plain or patterned general purpose field tiles.

Listello or **slip tiles** are long, narrow tiles,
which are either flat or rounded. They are
found in Victorian or Edwardian ranges and
can be used above or below the dado to
create a deeper border. Alternatively, you can
use a row of listello tiles between plain and
patterned field tiles before finishing off
with a dado.

BUYING TIPS

❖ **Choose with care** – tiling is semi-permanent decoration. Removal is difficult and may involve replastering the wall beneath.

❖ **Consider the scale** – generally speaking, it's a good idea to use small tiles for small expanses of wall, and larger tiles where there is more space. Large tiles on a small section of wall look odd and usually involve a great deal of cutting. Small tiles can make a large area seem cluttered and, because more are needed, will probably be dearer (and certainly more time-consuming) than using a larger tile.

❖ **Take samples home** – never buy new tiles without taking several different types home, so that you can see how the colour or pattern looks with your kitchen furniture or bathroom suite.

And remember that colours can appear dramatically different under shop lighting. Look at the tiles in the room where they will be used, in both natural and artificial light, before making a final colour choice.

❖ **Special measurements** – if you plan to use decor tiles, mark crosses on the wall where they will be positioned, and count the number to see how many you need to buy. For border tiles, measure the width of the area. If you plan to use two different tiles divided by a border or dado, measure the two areas separately.

❖ **Buy sale or return** – never underestimate the amount of tiles you'll need, but as tiles are expensive, ask if it's possible to buy on a sale or return basis. Most DIY stores and tile shops will give credit for whole unused boxes.

◢ *Animal motif*
Raised pattern tiles such as these frogs are a fun way of adding interest to plain tiles.

◀ *Colour gradation*
The tiles from some ranges have an interesting gradation of colour not only from tile to tile but within individual tiles themselves. Colours vary from box to box within the same range – for a good blend of colours mix up tiles from different boxes.

◀ *Victorian panel*
Victorian tiles can often be picked up in junk shops. Alternatively, there are many good modern reproductions. Build up a collection of favourites to create a multi-coloured panel for your wall.

▼ *Fireplace tiles*
This modern version of a late Victorian design is repeated in the hearth, and makes the fireplace eyecatching even during the summer months. Special fireplace tiles are made to withstand extreme heat.

▲ *Diagonal style*
Rows of different patterned tiles from the same handpainted Mexican range look effective when laid diagonally.

SETTING OUT

Setting out is the first stage of putting your tiling plan into action. Doing this properly ensures that cut tiles fall neatly on either side of the area to be tiled and that your tiles are positioned squarely. This is of critical importance to achieving a good finish.

Normally you fit tiles working upwards from the edge of a bath, the rim of a shower tray, a kitchen worktop, the top of a skirting board or the floor, all of which are likely to be too uneven to use as a base. So your first job is to draw a horizontal baseline which ensures that every row of tiles is level. Then you fix a straight batten along this line to support the first row of tiles.

You also need to set the width of the end columns on either side of the tiled area. Mark out each wall so that as far as possible you avoid cut tiles at external corners and at the sides of windows. Where cuts are required at both ends of a wall, find its midpoint and measure out from here so that each end column is even and, preferably, not less than half a tile in width.

HOW MANY TILES?

Find the area in square metres of each surface to be covered by multiplying its height by its width. Add the areas together and multiply by the number of tiles of your chosen design it takes to cover a square metre – this information is generally supplied on the packaging. Allow an extra five per cent for wastage.

If you have an exposed edge or edges to your tiling area, make sure you have enough suitable edging tiles, with rounded or glazed edges, unless you are using angled, universal tiles or fitting an edge trim.

1 Marking a guideline Using a straightedge and spirit level, draw a line right round the bottom of the area to be tiled, approximately a tile's width above where the lowest tiles are to finish.

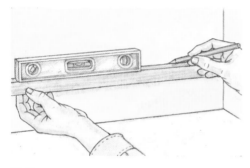

2 Drawing the baseline Take one tile and, holding it level with the base of the area to be tiled, mark the point where it rises highest above the guideline. Add 3mm (⅛in) to allow for the width of a grout line and draw the baseline round the bottom of the area to be tiled at this height, parallel to the guideline.

3 Fitting the support battens At 30cm (1ft) intervals, partly drive masonry nails into lengths of batten so that the points just show through. Position the top edge of one length of batten along the baseline and drive the nails into the wall until they hold, but no further than necessary – you will need to remove the batten later. Continue fitting battens along the baseline.

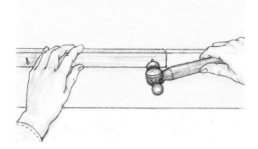

4 Positioning the end columns With your marking stick, work out where the last columns of whole tiles end on either side. Use a plumb line to draw vertical lines at these points.

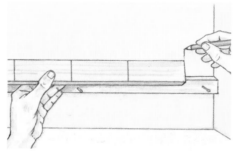

5 Fitting vertical battens Fix further lengths of batten, at right angles to the first, along the outside of the vertical lines, as in step 3. Check that the battens are vertical with a spirit level.

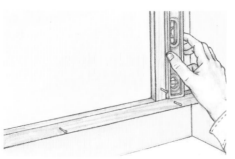

FITTING THE TILES

The tiles are fitted in horizontal rows from the bottom of the area to be tiled upwards. Work over a small area of the wall at a time so the tile adhesive does not dry out before you have a chance to embed the tiles.

1 **Fitting the first row** Spread about 1 sq m (1 sq yd) of tiling adhesive on the wall, using a notched spreader to leave it in ridges. Fix the first tile in the corner of the two battens. Continue fitting the tiles building up three or four rows at a time. With square-edged tiles, bed plastic spacers in the adhesive between the tiles; for tiles with angled edges or spacer lugs, push them up against one another.

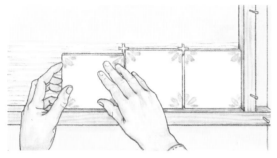

2 **Releasing the battens** Continue applying blocks of adhesive and tiles between the battens. Leave to set for an hour, then slide a knife blade along the batten edges to clear the joints. Remove the battens by pulling out the nails with pincers. Measure and cut tiles to fit the gaps and then fix them in place with tile adhesive.

◩ *A simple chequerboard pattern of yellow and deep green tiles is an effective choice for the walls of a utility room.*

3 **Grouting the tiles** Leave the tiles to set, usually for 12 hours. Cover the surrounding area. Apply and finish the grout and seal any gaps along the adjoining bath edge, shower tray or worktop with sealant.

◀ *Topiary trees are the unusual subject for the tiles of this kitchen splashback. Using a border tile means that two complete tiles fit in each vertical row, while a third tile needs a little cutting to fill in the gap under the dish-drying rack.*

Positioning a band of border tiles at window level all round the room enhances the proportions of the whole room. The edges of the window recess are neatened with a double-edge trim strip. Tiling the deep windowsill provides an extra storage surface.

CUTTING TILES

Generally, on a run of tiles along a wall, you will need to cut the tiles at each end to fit the area. When tiling a bath surround or the area behind a kitchen worktop, there should be no need for anything other than straight cuts which are quite simple to make.

A tile-cutting jig is the best way to make straight cuts parallel to the sides of the tiles. The jig has a built-in marking gauge which you set to the width of the gap to be filled before cutting; it automatically allows for the width of one grout line.

However, because a tile-cutting jig can only hold the tile to be cut squarely, you cannot use it to score diagonal cuts on the tile. To fill slanting gaps, you have to mark the tile by hand with a felt-tip pen, then score it with a handheld tile cutter against a straightedge.

1 **Sizing up the cut** Check that the space for a cut tile is uniform by measuring it top and bottom using the jig. If it is, you can use the jig to cut the tile. If not, transfer the measurements directly to the tile and make allowance for the grout line.

2 **Cutting the tile** *In a jig:* position the tile in the jig. Holding the tile and jig steady with one hand, line up the tile cutting tool in the guide and draw it firmly along the slot towards you. *By hand:* to cut a tile to fit a non-uniform gap, join the marks on the tile with a ruler and felt-tip pen. Use a hand cutter along a metal straightedge to score the tile surface.

3 **Splitting the tile** Grip the tile between the jaws of the cutting tool, with the jaws directly over the scored line. Hold the free side of the tile with your other hand, and squeeze gently with the tool to snap. Check the fit and smooth the cut edge with a tile file.

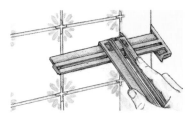

TILING CORNERS

Almost every tiling job involves turning a corner at some point. Prepare yourself for tackling corners during your planning and setting out.

Fitting into internal corners At internal corners, overlap one set of cut edges on to another. Plan in advance which way to arrange the overlap, and allow for a grout line.

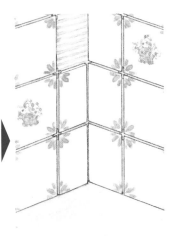

Fitting round external corners (1) You can finish external corners with a double-edge trim strip. Bed the strip in the adhesive, then simultaneously fix both columns of tiles so you can align them. You can use a single-edge trim strip for finishing off an exposed edge to a tiled area, especially when using plain-edged tiles.

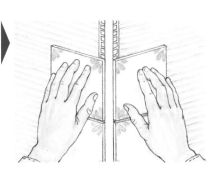

Fitting round external corners (2) Instead of using trim strip, overlap the adjacent tiles, making sure that the overlapping edge is glazed or rounded.

Wall tiling essentials

Ceramic tiles make an attractive, long-lasting covering for bathroom and kitchen walls.

With the right tools and materials, and careful planning and preparation, tiling a smooth, level wall is a straightforward job. The equipment needed for tiling is readily available from DIY stores. Always work in a well ventilated room when tiling, and wear gloves when handling grout and adhesive if your skin is at all sensitive.

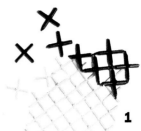

1

Tiling tools and materials

Tile adhesive sticks the tiles to the wall and comes ready to use in tubs. Check the tub for how much you will need. There are various kinds. Standard PVA based adhesives are only partly water resistant but are quite suitable for most walls and basin or sink splashbacks. Water resistant, acrylic-based adhesives are more expensive but are best for shower cubicles and bath splashbacks. Heat resistant adhesives are essential where temperatures are unusually high, such as around fires and cookers.

A notched adhesive spreader (3) furrows the adhesive, ensuring an even thickness. Sometimes one is supplied with the adhesive.

Grout fills the gaps between tiles.

Ready mixed grouts are acrylic based and come in tubs.

Powder grouts, which are cement based, come in bags for mixing with water and are slightly easier to apply.

Standard grout is white, but you can buy it in a range of colours. Alternatively you can buy special grout paint. Ordinary grout is reasonably water resistant and quite suitable for showers and splashbacks, though fully water resistant grout is available.

A grout spreader (2) has a rubber blade to spread the grout into the gaps between the tiles.

A grout joint finisher is a cheap plastic tool for firming the grout into place and giving it a smooth finish. Alternatively you can use a piece of 6mm (¼in) wooden dowel or the blunt end of a round pencil.

Tile spacers (1) are small plastic crosses for spacing square edged tiles – the commonest type. Some tiles already have bevelled edges or built-in spacer lugs to create a uniform gap.

Plastic edging or finishing strip in various colours is available to round off the exposed edges of outer tiles, though some tile ranges have special border and corner tiles with glazed edges.

Plastic sealing strip gives a watertight seal where tiles join a worktop, bath or basin. It is sold in 1.8m (6ft) lengths.

Silicone or acrylic sealant in a choice of colours comes in cartridge form and is an alternative to plastic sealing strip.

A tile cutter (6) scores the glazed surface of a tile, so the tile snaps easily and cleanly along the scored line. *An all-in-one tile cutter* (8) has a lever that trims and snaps in one action.

A tile saw (7) makes curved cuts for tiling around pipes and other obstructions.

A tile file (5) smooths the edges of cut tiles.

Tile nibblers (4) whittle away strips of tile too narrow to be snapped off.

2

3

4

5

Other equipment

For a professional finish you may also need:

A length of narrow timber to use as a gauging rod. Mark tile widths plus grouting spaces on it so that you can plan the positioning of the tiles.

Two wooden battens to fix to the wall to help you position the first column and the first row of tiles accurately.

A hammer and some masonry nails to secure the battens to the wall.

A level which shows the true vertical as well as horizontal, to position the battens correctly and check the alignment of the tiles regularly.

6

7

8

Preparing to tile

Preparing the wall

Make sure the wall is clean, flat, dry and firm. Plywood, blockboard and plasterboard need to be properly braced so they won't flex or warp. Don't attempt to tile on hardboard – it flexes too much – or chipboard, especially in bathrooms and around kitchen sinks, because it swells when wet causing the tiles to lift. If in doubt take expert advice.

After preparing the wall, remove obstructions if possible. Shaver and power points look better if the tiling fits behind them – isolate the supply and loosen fixing screws. If necessary, get an electrician to do this.

Tiling on plaster

Bare plaster Run a wooden batten over the wall, mark any bumps or depressions and level them off. Allow new plaster to dry for at least a month. Seal plaster with a PVA solution.

Wallcoverings Remove all old wallcoverings, even those which are firmly stuck down. Rake out any loose plaster, fill and level the surface. Fill and level any deep cracks.

Paint Remove any flaking paint and old wallplugs, and fill any cracks and holes. Wash the wall with (sugar) soap if the paint is dirty, then rub down with wet and dry abrasive paper.

Tiling on tiles

Existing tiles are a good base for new tiling, but the old tiles must be firmly fixed and perfectly flat. To ensure new tiles will adhere well, wash the old tiles to remove grease and dirt, then score the glazed surface with a tile cutter.

Half tiled wall (A) To tile a whole wall that has been half tiled, level the two sections by having plasterboard fitted to the untiled area, and filling any gaps between the two.

Cracked tiles (B) Fill and level any superficial cracks on tiles that are firmly fixed to the wall.

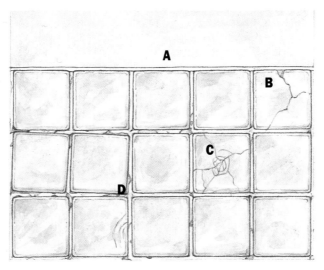

Loose tiles (D) Carefully lever off all loose tiles and either stick them – or new ones – firmly back on with tile adhesive, or level the gap with filler.

1 Broken tiles (C) Breaking up Tap firmly with a small hammer on a cloth pad held over the broken tile to break up the surface. To protect yourself from sharp edges you may want to wear goggles and work gloves when handling damaged tiles.

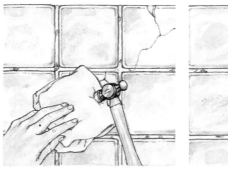

2 Chipping out Working from the centre outward, chip out the damaged tile with an old chisel.

TILING A SPLASHBACK

*Tiling a simple splashback on the wall above a basin or sink
is a perfect opportunity to try out your tiling skills. The result is a surface
that looks good and is practical and long lasting.*

With the help of modern tools and materials, tiling is a simple, satisfying job. If you haven't done any tiling before, a splashback is the ideal place to start, because you can get a feel for the technique without having to cut out difficult shapes.

A splashback can be a single row of tiles, or consist of several rows. Look at catalogues, magazines and shop displays to get an idea of the types of tiles available. Decide if you want plain or patterned tiles, or a mixture of both. Patterned tiles cost more, so you might opt for mainly plain tiles with a few patterned ones in groups or at random to liven them up. You can often buy small quantities of discontinued patterned tiles at a discount price, while junk shops or house clearances can be sources of beautiful old patterned tiles.

Also consider decorative border tiles, which come in many depths so you may not have to cut tiles to fit the space. Manufacturers often supply border tiles specially designed for a particular tile range, but you can choose any of the right size and thickness that you think complement the main body of the splashback.

A professional finish is within easy reach if you start with a simple project such as a splashback. Matching tiles to wallcoverings adds style, while border tiles top and bottom make for pleasing symmetry.

TILING THE EASY WAY

To be sure that your tiles stay up in place permanently and look really good, you must first take the time to prepare the wall thoroughly so that it is as clean and even as possible. You can stick tiles straight on to paint and plaster, and even on to old tiles, but not on to paper and other wallcoverings, so you must always remove these first.

After preparing the wall, work out exactly how you are going to position the tiles. Usually this means tiling outward from the middle of the wall, so that any cut tiles or gaps at the ends are the same size. Try not to use cut tiles that are less than a third of their original width. Likewise, try not to leave narrow gaps. Sit the first row of tiles against the basin if the edge is straight and level, otherwise use a wooden batten to support the first row and cut tiles to fit round the basin later.

▶ *The lightly patterned white tiles on this handsome kitchen sink splashback make for a happy alliance of the decorative and the functional.*

◤ *A few handpainted, floral pattern tiles scattered at random enliven a panel of plain white tiles. With fresh cut flowers to match, the overall effect is light and summery.*

POSITIONING THE TILES

Starting at the mid point First work out the best way to position the tiles. Usually they look best laid either side of the mid point.

Centring on the mid point If starting at the mid point doesn't work, try laying out the tiles with the first one centred over the mid point instead.

Using a batten If the back of the basin is shaped, nail a batten to the wall one tile height above the rim. Check it's level and leave nail heads protruding for easy removal. Tile above batten, then remove it and fill in base row, cutting tiles to fit.

Marking the start Use a spirit level to draw a true vertical at the point where the tiling is to start.

STICKING THE TILES

1 Applying the adhesive Scoop the adhesive out of the tub and press it on to the wall. Draw the spreader across so the teeth ridge the adhesive to a level thickness. Apply enough adhesive to position up to six tiles in the first row. Make sure you can still see the mid point line – scrape away a little adhesive if necessary.

▼ Matching black and white accessories to border tiles shows how classy plain white tiles can be.

2 Positioning the first tile Holding the tile at an angle of 45° to the wall, align it with the vertical starting line and press it firmly back into the adhesive. Check that it is level using the spirit level.

3 Adding further tiles Bed spacers into the adhesive at the top and bottom of the first tile and position next tile. Continue spacing and fixing the row. Leave any cut tiles until later, but scrape off any excess adhesive before it sets.

4 Checking the fit Before adding further rows, check the tiles in the first row are flush with one another. Press in any that are sticking out. Prise out any that have sunk too deep and put more adhesive on the wall before rebedding them.

CUTTING

On a splashback there should be no need for anything other than simple straight cuts, unless the wash basin has a sculptured rim. If you have a few tiles to cut, it may be worth investing in an all-in-one cutting tool, like the one shown below, which both scores and snaps the tile – you simply position the tile carefully, score along the appropriate line, then snap the tile cleanly.

Alternatively, using a metal rule as a straight edge, score along the glazed side of the tile with a cutter, then put a matchstick under the tile along the scored line and press down firmly on both sides to snap the tile cleanly. Test the fit of each cut tile and file the cut edges smooth.

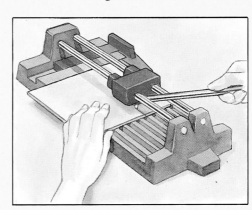

FINISHING OFF

When you have completed the first row of tiles you can continue sticking further rows to the wall in the same way, then leave them to set overnight before grouting the gaps.

1 Grouting the tiles Load a small amount of grout on to the flexible spreader and draw it across the gaps between the tiles, forcing it well in. Use a damp sponge to wipe off any surplus as you complete an area of about six tiles at a time.

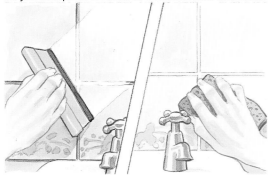

2 Finishing the joints When the grout begins to harden, smooth down the joints with a joint finisher to remove excess grout and leave the surface slightly concave.

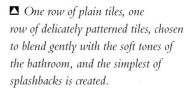 *One row of plain tiles, one row of delicately patterned tiles, chosen to blend gently with the soft tones of the bathroom, and the simplest of splashbacks is created.*

3 Cleaning the tiles Wipe off any stray grout left on the tiles, then polish the tile surface with a dry cloth.

4 Applying sealant Seal the gap along the join between the bottom row of tiles and the basin or sink with sealant. Squeeze the sealant from the tube with an even pressure and push the tube away from you along the gap. Smooth the sealant down lightly by drawing a moistened finger along the join, then leave it to set. Trim off excess sealant with a sharp blade.

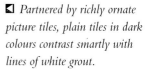 *Partnered by richly ornate picture tiles, plain tiles in dark colours contrast smartly with lines of white grout.*

A border of dainty gold tesserae – small mosaic squares – adds a grand flourish to this handsome mirror. The fine beading between the mirror and mosaic is gilded to match the tesserae.

MOSAIC APPEAL

Let the art of mosaic introduce rich colour and flowing pattern into your home, on walls, floors, furniture, and accessories which you can either buy or create yourself.

The art of mosaic – forming decorative designs with small pieces of glass, ceramic or any other material – has flourished for centuries: mosaic floors, walls, furniture and artefacts are to be found at many ancient sites, testifying to mosaic's strength and durability as well as its timeless appeal.

As our ancestors knew, every home benefits from the infusion of colour and pattern that mosaic decoration brings – whether over whole walls and floors, as splashbacks, friezes or worksurfaces, or to embellish furniture and accessories such as table tops, lampbases, mirror and picture frames.

You'll find a range of mosaic items in shops, but it is highly satisfying, inexpensive and easier than you would think to create your own. You can either use tesserae – small squares of mosaic glass, available from art and craft shops – as shown in the pictures here, or improvize with pieces of broken-up crockery, or even pebbles, shells and beads. The beauty of mosaic design is that it can be as small or large-scale as you like – the tiny mosaic fragments can even be used as shelf edgings – so you can adapt the size of your mosaic project to suit the time you have available. For a witty finishing touch, set off the real thing with mosaic-print fabrics.

◀ *Shimmering glass tesserae* in shades of copper, bronze and emerald are stuck side by side along the front edge of these shelves, defining their unusual curving lines. You can quickly and easily stick the tesserae in place using a glue gun.

▶ *Eye-catching blocks of mosaic* on the front of the work platform and around the corner window add colour, texture and a modern edge to this mellow-toned kitchen.

▽ *Cool blue*, perfectly square tesserae cover these bathroom walls and floor, giving a hardwearing, waterproof finish that's also the height of chic.

▽ *Simple but effective designs* are easy to create with tesserae tiles – like the symmetrical black and white pattern on this kitchen splashback. It's a good idea to work out your design on squared paper before you stick any tiles in place.

Index

ACKNOWLEDGEMENTS

Photographs

7 Abode UK, 8-9 Eaglemoss Publications/Steve Tanner, 10(t) Crown Paints, 10(b) Eaglemoss Publications/Steve Tanner, 11 IPC Magazines/Robert Harding Syndication, 12-13 Eaglemoss Publications/Martin Chaffer, 14 IPC Magazines/Robert Harding Syndication, 15 Eaglemoss Publications/Graham Rae, 16, 17 IPC Magazines/Robert Harding Syndication, 18(t) Mira Showers, 18(c,b) Eaglemoss Publications/Graham Rae, 19 Crown Paints, 20-21 Eaglemoss Publications/Steve Tanner, 22(t) EWA/Nadia McKenzie, 22(bl) Ikea, 22(br) IPC Magazines/Robert Harding Syndication, 23 EWA/Andreas von Einsiedel, 24-25, 26 Eaglemoss Publications/Steve Tanner, 27 EWA/Brian Harrison, 28-29 Eaglemoss Publications/Simon Page-Ritchie, 30(t) IPC Magazines/Robert Harding Syndication, 30(br) Eaglemoss Publications/Simon Page-Ritchie, 31 EWA/Andreas von Einsiedel, 32-33, 34 Eaglemoss Publications/Simon Page-Ritchie, 41-42 Eaglemoss Publications/Graham Rae, 45 English Stamp Company, 46, 47, 48(tl,tr) Eaglemoss Publications/Graham Rae, 48(bl) English Stamp Company, 48(br) DoehetZelf Holland, 49 IPC Magazines/Robert Harding Syndication, 50(tl) Elrose Products, 50 (bl) EWA/Shona Wood, 50(tr,cr,br) Woman & Home/PWA International, 51 Eaglemoss Publications/Adrian Taylor, 53 EWA/Spike Powell, 54 Eaglemoss Publications/Steve Tanner, 55 Eaglemoss Publications/Simon Page-Ritchie, 56(tr) EWA/Spike Powell, 56(cl) Sharps Bedrooms, 56(bl) Eaglemoss Publications/Simon Page-Ritchie, 56(br) IPC Magazines/Robert Harding Syndication, 57 LG Harris & Company, 58-59 EWA/Rodney Hyett, 60 EWA/Dennis Stone, 61 Eaglemoss Publications/Graham Rae, 62 Crown Paints, 63 IPC Magazines/Robert Harding Syndication, 64(t) EWA/Rodney Hyett, 64(bl)

Crown Paints, 64(bc,br) Eaglemoss Publications/Graham Rae, 65 Romo Fabrics, 67 Sanderson, 68 Eaglemoss Publications/Graham Rae, 69, 71 EWA/Andreas von Einsiedel, 72 Anna French, 74 Eaglemoss Publications/Iain Bagwell, 75 IPC Magazines/Robert Harding Syndication, 76-77(l) Eaglemoss Publications/Mark Wood, 77(br), 78(bl) Shand Kydd 78(r) Eaglemoss Publications/Mark Wood, 79, 80(t,cl) Shand Kydd, 80(cr) IPC Magazines/Robert Harding Syndication, 80(b) Crown Wallcoverings, 81 Laura Ashley Home, 82(bl) Fablon, 82-83(t) Sanderson, 82-83(b) Laura Ashley Home, 84 Texas Homecare, 85 EWA/Andreas von Einsiedel, 86 IPC Magazines/Robert Harding Syndication, 87 EWA/Spike Powell, 88(t) Marie Claire IdÇes/Schwartz/Chastres/Lancrenon, 88(bl,br), 89 Eaglemoss Publications/Simon Page-Ritchie, 91, 92(t,bl) IPC Magazines/Robert Harding Syndication, 92(br) Abode UK, 93, 94(tl,tr) IPC Magazines/Robert Harding Syndication, 94(bl) EWA/Spike Powell, 94(br) Ariadne Holland, 95 Marie O'Hara, 96(tl,tr) IPC Magazines/Robert Harding Syndication, 96(bl) DoehetZelf Holland, 96(br) Paul Ryan, 97 IPC Magazines/Robert Harding Syndication, 98(tl) Sue Atkinson, 98(tr) Eaglemoss Publications/Martin Chaffer, 98(bl,br) Eaglemoss Publications/Simon Page-Ritchie, 99, 100(tl,bl) IPC Magazines/Robert Harding Syndication, 100(tr) Eaglemoss Publications/Mark Wood, 100(br) EWA/Nick Carter, 101 Eaglemoss Publications/Steve Tanner, 102(t) IPC Magazines/Robert Harding Syndication, 102(cl) EWA/Spike Powell, 102(cr) Eaglemoss Publications/Martin Chaffer, 102(b) Eaglemoss Publications/Simon Page-Ritchie, 103, 104(t,bl) IPC Magazines/Robert Harding Syndication, 104(br) EWA/David Giles, 105, 106(t) Blue Hawk Ltd, 107(br) IPC Magazines/Robert Harding Syndication, 108(t) Vencel Resil, 108(b) Eaglemoss Publications/Simon Page-Ritchie, 109 IPC Magazines/Robert Harding Syndication, 110(t) EWA/Rodney Hyett, 110(b) World's End Tiles, 111(tl) Marlborough Tiles, 111(tr) Woman &

Home/PWA International, 111(b) Fired Earth, 112(tr) Eaglemoss Publications/Graham Rae, 112(bl) Brookman Kitchens, 112-113(b) Fired Earth, 113(t) Paul Ryan, 113(br) Stovax Ltd, 114(t) Fired Earth, 114(bl) Paul Ryan, 114(br) Eaglemoss Publications/Graham Rae, 115 H&R Johnson, 116-117(b) Osborne & Little, 117(tr) Fired Earth, 118 H&R Johnson, 119, 121 Eaglemoss Publications/Graham Rae, 122(bl) Fired Earth, 122-123(tr) Laura Ashley Home, 123(bl), 124(tr) Eaglemoss Publications/Graham Rae, 124(bl) IPC Magazines/Robert Harding Syndication, 125 Marie Claire Maison/Morel/Postic, 126(tl) IPC Magazines/Robert Harding Syndication, 126(tr,bl) EWA/Rodney Hyett, 126(br) EWA/Tom Leighton.

Illustrations

8-10 Sally Holmes, 12-14 Tig Sutton, 20 Sally Holmes, 24-26 Coral Mula, 28-30 Sally Holmes, 32-33 Coral Mula, 35-36 Ian Sidaway, 37-38 Sally Holmes, 43-44 Ian Sidaway, 52 Sally Holmes, 54-56 Coral Mula, 58-60 Sally Holmes, 62-63 Coral Mula, 66-68 Tig Sutton, 70-72 Sally Holmes, 74 Coral Mula, 77-78 Sally Holmes, 82-84 Aziz Khan, 84(br) Stan North, 86-87 Sally Holmes, 89-90 David Ashby, 106-107 Coral Mula, 116-118, 120 Sally Holmes, 122-124 Tig Sutton.